T0013301

PARENT
AND
CHILD
The Two-Person Family

Kathleen M. Waddington

BALBOA.
PRESS
A DIVISION OF HAY HOUSE

Copyright © 2017 Kathleen M. Waddington.

All rights reserved. No part of this book may be used or reproduced by any means, graphic, electronic, or mechanical, including photocopying, recording, taping or by any information storage retrieval system without the written permission of the author except in the case of brief quotations embodied in critical articles and reviews.

Balboa Press books may be ordered through booksellers or by contacting:

Balboa Press
A Division of Hay House
1663 Liberty Drive
Bloomington, IN 47403
www.balboapress.com.au
1 (877) 407-4847

Because of the dynamic nature of the Internet, any web addresses or links contained in this book may have changed since publication and may no longer be valid. The views expressed in this work are solely those of the author and do not necessarily reflect the views of the publisher, and the publisher hereby disclaims any responsibility for them.

The author of this book does not dispense medical advice or prescribe the use of any technique as a form of treatment for physical, emotional, or medical problems without the advice of a physician, either directly or indirectly. The intent of the author is only to offer information of a general nature to help you in your quest for emotional and spiritual well-being. In the event you use any of the information in this book for yourself, which is your constitutional right, the author and the publisher assume no responsibility for your actions.

Any people depicted in stock imagery provided by Thinkstock are models, and such images are being used for illustrative purposes only.
Certain stock imagery © Thinkstock.

Print information available on the last page.

ISBN: 978-1-5043-0713-0 (sc)
ISBN: 978-1-5043-0714-7 (e)

Balboa Press rev. date: 06/26/2017

To my father 'Boysie,' whose love has no boundaries.
You're always present in my heart and soul, beyond the realms of this life.

Contents

Introduction ix

PART 1: TWO IN A FAMILY

How Did This Single Parenting Thing Happen to Me?............................1
My Story 5
Living as a Two-Member Family 10
Living in the Moment.. 14
Family Dynamics 20
Keeping the Peace 28

PART 2: PERSEVERANCE

Questions Raised... 35
Time Spent Together 39
Networking: Create Your Community 48
Filtering Advice 52
Conflict of Roles... 56
Discipline 61
Talking about Sex... 64
The Drug Issue.. 66

PART 3: BUILDING INNER STRENGTH

Co-Sleeping 71
Managing Stress.. 74

The Pursuit of Happiness 86

Utilize the Power of the Mind 103

Align your Energy 110

Enhancing Confidence 116

PART 4: MOVING FORWARD

Dealing with Illness, Death and the Barbed Wire of Life 125

Isolation 130

Letting Go 134

Purpose 140

Reflection 146

Conclusion 151

Introduction

This book is a product of my own experiences, insight gained from many single parent friends, and inspiration and wisdom obtained from knowledge acquired along the way.

I don't profess to be an expert in adult or child psychology. I have merely gathered information through living my own personal life and through the observation of others. In my profession as a health care practitioner, l have also undertaken research on particular subjects that add substance to my story.

When referring to others, I will change names to protect peoples' identities.

As the reader, you may be a new parent or a parent of a young child, teenager, or young adult. This book is intended to be of relevance to you as a parent/guardian of either gender through all stages of your parenting life.

I don't think that I am a better parent than anyone else. I only strive to be the best I can be. I have made many mistakes along the way. I consider them to be lessons learnt. There are things I wish I had done differently, and I expect that will continue throughout my parenting days.

A two-person family may be the product of circumstances or choice. Whichever it may be, this family presents a certain set of challenges— some of which you may already be equipped to deal with and others that will simply surprise you.

In this book, l refer to the family as consisting of parent and child, whether that constitutes mother and child, father and child, or even grandparent or other sole guardian and child. The family may have been formed as a product of divorce, separation, death, adoption, family illness, or personal choice. Variants to this two-person family may include one spouse working and living away from home and older siblings having moved out and living elsewhere.

If you are a single parent or guardian with more than one child, I am sure that many life situations and experiences discussed in this book are also very relevant to you.

I hope that I can impart some of the knowledge I have gained as a single parent with one child to help others through their individual journeys.

Whether by choice or the result of an unpredictable predicament, heading a two-person family is probably not what you anticipated as a youngster looking toward the future.

Perhaps as a child growing up you planned to have a conventional family of your own and that plan commenced but was stumped in the making by illness, separation, divorce, or death of a partner. Or perhaps you found yourself of a certain mature age, where the traditional family scenario was no longer obtainable, so you decided to go it alone, to have one or more children on your own and develop a family that way. Maybe you have taken on the role of sole guardian as a relative or friend of the family when circumstances have warranted. Or perhaps you have undertaken foster parenting.

Parenting is, by no means, a straightforward, easy task, no matter how the family is structured. The way we parent depends on many factors— how we ourselves were parented, our individual conditioning and beliefs, our observations of how others parent, comments and advice from well-intentioned family members and friends, professional advice, and the wisdom gained from our own parenting experiences and research. Taking all of this into account, our particular style of parenting will be a derivative of combined forces.

There are many parallels between dual and single parenting. Each has its separate challenges. I believe that, in all circumstances, there are similarities and uniqueness. Without discrediting styles of parenting in any given family, I would like to focus on what particular exceptions may present in the one-parent family.

Your family may consist of shared parenting. Many different variations of this exist. Although your child may live with you, he or she may also spend some time with the other parent. The degree of influence you as a parent have and the overall parent-child relationship the two of you form will depend on the quality and quantity of time you spend together. In cases where the other parent is completely absent from the child's life or living in another country or faraway town, he or she may have limited, if any, input into the child's upbringing.

Whichever category of single parenting you fit, consider yourself a special person. You have been uniquely chosen by the universe to care and parent your child, mostly or entirely on your own. Whilst this may seem daunting at times, think of it as an opportunity to bring out the best in your abilities.

PART 1

Two in a Family

How Did This Single Parenting Thing Happen to Me?

I really didn't expect anything out of the ordinary to happen in my life. I cruised along, believing that everything would go along according to what was customary. My plans were typical of a girl growing up—a career, marriage, children. I was well aware that certain things happen to people, causing a derailment in their lives; I just assumed I wouldn't be one of those people.

In many cases, single parenting is the result of unforeseen circumstances. Even if a person chooses to go it alone, most of the time, his or her intention would likely have been to dual parent if the situation presented itself. There are many paths in life. Single parenting is one of them—perhaps not one we single parents would have willingly chosen, but it presented itself to us anyway.

Single parenting can conjure up an array of emotions that need to be dealt with. You may find yourself a single parent as the result of a failed relationship. If so, you could feel resentful or embarrassed that your choice of a partner was a poor one, wondering if maybe you were oblivious to warning signs that shone like a neon light to everyone else. It could be that your relationship just fizzled out; you grew apart from one another, and cohabiting didn't work for you anymore. In the case of losing your partner through death, you could be dealing with resentment that the person didn't get to live a full life and share in the family life—and left you and your child to go on living without him or her. Or your life may have been travelling a different path when it was interrupted by the need to take on guardianship of another person's child—a child you otherwise wouldn't have had sole responsibility for. Even if you willingly chose to parent alone, you may feel overwhelmed by the enormity of the task at hand. There are many possible scenarios that lead someone to becoming a single parent.

Finding yourself in any of the above unforeseen circumstances can be unsettling. There will be new adjustments necessary that may introduce added stressors to an already stressful situation.

What helped me tremendously after my separation was to deal with one thing at a time. Despite having so much on my plate—getting counselling, finding suitable childcare, dealing with the court system, working, finding a place of my own to live, and so forth—l knew that l would be much less stressed if l just took baby steps. After all, the worst-case scenario was always that l would go to bed at night, get up the next day, and then deal again with what l needed to that day. Life went on; this wasn't going to kill me. l would wake up the next day, refreshed and ready to tackle the next thing on my to-do list. Whenever l felt down, the assurance that there was a new day ahead, would always comfort me. Besides, we all need our sleep to sort things out in our minds, to tidy up our files and create new ones. We also need to allow ourselves time, however much is required, to get through our daily tasks without feeling pressured or guilty.

I eventually ticked off everything on my list. I grieved my loss, took on a new path, and finally came to an acceptance. I am not saying that this was an easy feat. There were some days when I slacked off, unable to do anything but indulge in my emotions. Looking back, I believe that was a necessary part of the process. Reflecting on some trials and tribulations along the way, l can now see how they have blended into my pool of life experiences.

Providing you have some sort of plan of action in place and you don't allow yourself to get stuck in any negative emotions, you will be able to move forward, and things will come together eventually. You just need to give yourself the time and space required. It's no good beating yourself up for things you haven't done or lingering on emotions you thought you had put a lid on.

Feelings that surface won't go away if you try to suppress them. Allow your emotions to play out. Imagine yourself as your best friend, giving you some advice. You would want to help your friend, wouldn't you? In reality, you are your best friend! You would, I am sure, give your friend permission to express and feel emotions. You would also seek ways to comfort your friend by suggesting ways of pampering him or her. Treat yourself as you would your friend. By taking some time out for yourself; focusing on your needs; and indulging in some rest, relaxation, and recreational activities, you will come back refreshed and determined. Even if you feel there is so much to be done, allow yourself time out. You will be a much better parent for it!

It can be very difficult to put 100 per cent into parenting during a time of turmoil. During the early days of grieving and adjusting to new circumstances in the event of losing a partner, or even in the event of losing your freedom, you may just want to focus on yourself. It is difficult to scrounge up any energy for anything else, let alone your beloved child. Your child needs emotional comfort, reassurance, and stability, and meeting your child's needs can be an uphill battle for you when your resources are drained. At these times, it is a good idea to take advantage of family and friends to ensure that you have the space you need. If you haven't a family or social network or if you have relocated and don't have anyone nearby to take on some childcare or with whom you can talk over the telephone, then I suggest you contact a parent helpline. The person on the other end of the line will be able to give you some support and may be able to refer you to other relevant associations.

Family and friends can be invaluable. They can take on some childcare, do some other chores for you, or provide a listening ear to help lessen your burdens and talk over your concerns.

Keeping your head above water may seem overwhelming when you become a newly single parent. There will be times when you feel you can't get enough air, and then there will be times of triumph and self-appreciation for what you have achieved. Take it step by step—take baby steps if you need to. Remember to be kind to yourself; allow your emotions to play out, accepting the tides of highs and lows. Ask for and accept help. Eventually, in your own time, you will make progress.

My Story

I came from a family of six, consisting of my mother and father, my older brother, me (the second eldest), and a younger brother and sister. We lived in a country town in a modest home, with varying pets from time to time.

By the age of five, l had planned what I wanted when I grew up. First of all, l wanted to become a nurse, and then I would marry (probably a doctor, as nurses married doctors on television) and then have ten children.

Well, l did become a nurse. My career path pretty much turned out as I planned. My personal life, on the other hand, turned in a very different direction from what l had anticipated.

I remember having a discussion with my mother as a young teenager on becoming a single mother. "That will never happen to me," I told her.

She responded, "I trust you, just not your hormones!"

At the time l thought that single parenting only happened to teenagers. Little did l know back then that, a few decades later, l would become a single parent as a middle-aged woman!

When I was a child, the only single parents I ever knew were teenage mothers or widowed women. In the 1970s, it was still commonplace for an "illegitimate" child to be disguised in a family as a younger sibling of the biological mother. There were three such cases among my classmates. One girl disappeared from school for a period of six months, supposedly with glandular fever. Rumours had it that she went away to have a baby.

My own family had its secrets. It wasn't until the age of sixteen that I learnt my father was one such child, camouflaged into the family as another sibling of his mother's. He grew up believing that his mother was his sister—until overhearing through gossip the truth of the matter at the tender age of eleven.

Divorce, separation, and children born out of wedlock weren't accepted back in those times like they are now. There was a stigma attached to them. People didn't have the means to separate as they do now, so they were more inclined to stay in unhealthy relationships. Talking about your private matters with family or friends was taboo. The marriage vows "until death do us part" were seriously adhered to, no matter what the circumstances. It was believed that separation would be detrimental to the children, when in fact it is now considered to be the healthier option in many situations.

In those days, you were pretty much considered an outcast if you didn't belong in the traditional nuclear family. If you were a product of an unwedded union, you were labelled a bastard child, and if you were the by-product of separation or divorce, you came from a broken family. If you were involved in a same-sex relationship, you were queer or otherwise dubbed a faggot, poofter, or lesbian. How could a person possibly adapt, let alone feel accepted in society when stereotyped in such a negative way?

Times are different now. We have a wider choice in terms of the types of family relationships we create. Our society now respects all unions— heterosexual or same-sex couples, married or not. With regard to having children, a single woman may now choose to have a child on her own. People are better educated and more accepting of failed relationships, and a wide variety of counselling services is available to suit individual needs.

Of course, not all relationships need to end if there are problems. Couples may be able to work through their difficulties with some counselling, and the family unit may remain intact. However, if the environment of the family is subject to constant disruption through abusive, violent, or addictive behaviour, then the family's overall well-being is at risk. Each member may be affected in some detrimental way, in which case separation is a healthier option.

I gave birth to my baby boy at the age of forty-two. Two years later, my relationship ended, and shortly after that, my son's father moved to another state.

For some time, l used to want for what l didn't have, envious of two-parented families with more than one child. After all, that had always been my childhood dream. I will admit that this would, at times, consume me, particularly in the first few years after my breakup. After my grieving, I wanted to think more positively about my situation, without wallowing in pity or regret. I had to make the best of my situation for the well-being of myself and my child. I decided to appreciate what l did have and focus on that.

I have come to believe that events, good and bad, happen in life for a greater purpose. Life presents us with many lessons to learn from. I believe that my ending up as a single parent to one child was in my life plan, governed by a greater power. Although it wasn't what l willingly chose or expected, it occurred anyway. Having this belief has enabled me to embrace my life as it is, accepting its challenges and, knowing within; that I have much to learn and gain from my own particular life story.

It did, however, take me some time to absorb my unexpected life journey. I had to adapt to my new circumstances.

The first thing l wanted to do after separating was to get on with life. I wanted it all behind me, and quickly. I figured that it would probably take around a month or two to feel better. That wasn't the case. I required more time.

I acknowledge that everyone has different and varying circumstances and that there are a lot of emotions to work through when you become a single parent. What we all have in common is a duty to raise our children to the best of our ability.

What I personally wanted and needed was some help. Although I appreciated physical help, topping my list was the need to seek out some professional assistance through counselling. I had one primary concern: How was I going to do this on my own? I wanted to be the best parent I could be. I knew that my ex-partner would probably have little input, if any, in any kind of parenting, and I needed some strategies to deal with forthcoming issues and questions from my child when they arose.

If I could work through my psychological state, I figured, other concerns would become less of a burden. After all, if your mental health is in check, you can better deal with other stressors.

I engaged in some professional counselling. My mind felt as if someone had thrown a bucket of glue over it. I needed to clear it so I could begin the process of moving on. I felt that l desperately needed some answers to my questions. However, not all of the required answers presented themselves instantaneously. On reflection, if they had, I would have been overloaded with information. With time and patience, the answers came to me. I was able to work through each stage as it presented itself, sometimes taking on advice previously given to me and working with that, and sometimes devising my own solutions.

It was important for me to be around family and friends whenever possible, so that I felt comforted and supported. This sometimes required travelling long distances. Being among those who love and care for you and your offspring enables you to gather the confidence and energy required for the tasks ahead. Of course, you will most likely receive an abundance of advice as well, requested or not! Nevertheless, you know that your loved ones' suggestions, even the unsolicited variety, are made with the best intentions, and you can decipher what is and isn't suited to your individual circumstances and needs.

I am still in the midst of raising my son, now a teenager. His other parent has no input or influence. This leaves me to sole parent as I see fit. You could think of this as being a disadvantage; I see it as not being subject to what could possibly be conflicting ideas and advice from the other parent. I love being a mother, a parent, albeit an only one. The challenge of single parenting has opened up so many channels in my life. I have discovered my strengths and unleashed my weaknesses. I have developed an independence l wouldn't have had l remained partnered. I have had to make decisions and accomplish tasks on my own without another parents' help, all of which brings a sense of personal satisfaction and growth.

I have had another relationship since the separation from my child's father, and I am now again single. At the moment, I'm happy with that. I'm open to another relationship in my life, although I am not actively looking for one just now.

Living as a Two-Member Family

As a newly separated person, 1 didn't feel like 1 was a part of a family anymore, particularly when I had just the one child. I felt in limbo. Part of me felt ensconced in family life, and yet another part of me felt single. I felt I didn't fit into the "norm," even though I was well aware that there were many others like me.

I knew that I needn't have felt this way. Nevertheless, it was how 1 felt. I can only attribute those feelings to my conditioned aspirations and expectations of how my life would pan out. My life turned in a very different direction than the one I'd imagined.

At first 1 used to hang around family and single friends. I didn't feel I constituted a family of my own, so I didn't feel comfortable attending events for "families." I wished that my family consisted of more than a mere two members. I was shy, embarrassed by my situation.

What 1 was missing was a sense of belonging. This only became apparent when I ventured out to meet other like situated people. I joined a single parents group and felt that I'd found a missing link. I could identify with these people. They were a wonderful support to me, as we all shared common circumstances. Our lifestyles were similar, and we often spent family evenings and weekends away together. Our children became very accustomed to socializing in family settings where one parent was the norm. Joining a single parents group helped me regain my confidence and self-esteem at a time when 1 felt disconnected in society. 1 needed to feel as though 1 slotted in somewhere comfortably. I wanted to share and compare my experiences with other single parents. Over time, as my child progressed through school and became involved in sports and extracurricular activities, a whole new world opened up. Needless to say, I've met many more single-parent families along the way.

Once l formed this association with my single parent friends, I could move on more confidently, knowing that my son and I were no less a family with our two members than any other. Having friends whose lives mirrored mine, really empowered me to overcome the belief that mine was only a half family. I began to feel more at ease being involved in social settings predominantly composed of nuclear families.

As a single-parent family, it is possible to feel ostracized by friends at times. Single friends may not invite you to social events, as they may think attending too difficult for you (in terms of affordability or the need to make childcare arrangements). Partnered friends may exclude you for similar reasons, or they may feel you could be hurt or sensitive to the fact that they are partnered and you are not. Perhaps it could be assumed that you would feel odd being the only one without a partner—that things wouldn't be even. When your friends sometimes leave you out, you shouldn't feel offended. I put it down to human nature. You could say that your friends are being careful, thoughtful of your situation, and you could turn things around by understanding this and being the one to instigate the invitations. Be mindful that you form friendships with people who appreciate you for who you are. Friendship bonds have nothing to do with your social settings.

There have been times I've wished I were the one parading around in the car with the numerous family stick figures stuck on the back windscreen. You know the ones—Dad holding up the barbecued sausage, Mum with the tennis racket, and three kids (usually also involved in extracurricular activities) and dog in tow. As wonderful as this family unit may appear, these images do not denote the real family involved in day-to-day living. Nor do these images depict the average family structure, given that there are so many variables. How easy it can be to dwell on and become envious of what these images portray—the "happy nuclear family."

In reality, though, we all have different family shapes, each bearing sometimes similar and sometimes different sets of challenges. As much as these images try to trick me into believing that "their life is better," I have come to an acceptance of my own family situation and its benefits. There can be so much more freedom in a smaller family. And when you desire more companionship, you can make your own family bigger by incorporating your extended family and/or widening your friendships. The grass isn't greener on the other side. There's green grass growing in all sorts of paddocks. Enjoy the paddock you're in!

To think that I was totally responsible for raising my child was rather frightening. I couldn't depend at all on my son's other parent. This was, at first, daunting—when I realized I had to make all the decisions by myself. I alone had to decide how to set up home, what childcare and schooling options were best, what kind of discipline would be most productive, what extracurricular activities to involve him in, and on and on.

Looking back now, it wasn't as difficult as I anticipated, largely because I didn't have to make all those decisions at once, and there were others I could rely on for help when necessary. When you don't have a partner to support or help you with some important decisions, there are plenty of other people you can obtain advice from, especially those who are themselves parents. In fact, you can take on another's advice and have the freedom to do as you wish with it, without the hassle of a partner's conflicting opinions or beliefs.

What about the isolation you may feel in a two-member family? I guess it feels different as you travel through the stages of your child's development. In your child's preschool years, you may feel stuck at home a lot. Even though you get plenty of enjoyment from the cuteness of your child, he or she is very demanding of your time. You can't get out of the house much, as your little one can't be left on his or her own. And there are sleep routines to consider. As your child grows and enters the school years his or her independence develops, which allows you a little more freedom and time alone. Time continues on, and the independence strengthens. As the young person continues to evolve, you begin to enjoy other assets of your child's being. The two of you develop some shared interests and engage in more mature conversations. During the adolescent years, your child will crave solitude and privacy, and the alone time you so desperately desired may suddenly become a little too much.

There will be times when you feel more isolated than others. There is no one else in the household to turn your attention on, no other companion with whom to spend time. Just know that these phases don't last. Things keep changing. If you think your household is a bit quiet, invite other children over for play dates, hangouts, or sleepovers. You could include some adult company for yourself. As the children are occupied, you will find it a good time to enjoy some quality companionship with friends of your own.

Even though you will be quite busy raising, caring for, and providing taxi service for your child throughout the years, it is very important that you maintain your friendships and resume a social life whenever time permits. Otherwise, when things turn full circle in your child's life (from dependant infancy to independent youth) you may feel at a loose end. You'll suddenly have an abundance of time on your hands—time you previously shared with your child.

Being a two-member household doesn't mean that you have to miss out on the liveliness present in a larger household. It just means you have to make adjustments to equal that atmosphere. Developing and maintaining a healthy network of friends can keep loneliness at bay during those quieter periods in life.

Living in the Moment

There is the past, the present, and the future. We can only live in the present, the now, the moment. The past is an important catalyst to present events. The future is the path ahead.

We can't change the past, so there is no point in dwelling on past events. We can't predict the future, so there's no use wasting time on worrying about it. What we have in front of us is the now—the moment we exist in life. If we can be present in the moment and appreciate the *now* times, we will develop a stronger sense of our inner being and what's important in our world as it is, without any hang ups or regrets about what "could have been," had we done this or that differently or made other choices.

Think back to when you were a child. All that existed was the moment. You didn't think too much about past events—unless you had a scratch on your leg, which reminded you that you fell from climbing a tree a few days back. You weren't capable of or interested in looking into what would be happening in your life in a week's time, let alone anything beyond that. You lived life as it presented itself. Now, look at yourself as an adult. You may be planning what you need to get done before the end of the day, tomorrow, or next week. Our minds don't sit still in the fast-paced world we live in, which interrupts our enjoyment of the present. Sure, we need to make forward plans so our lives run smoothly. However, it is in no way necessary that we become consumed by them—distracted from experiencing life as it happens. Nor is there any gain in rehashing what we should have said or done in the past.

Our thoughts are forever interrupting our experience of life, especially if we are experiencing stress, illness, worry, or grief—when our minds are in overdrive. We can become so completely lost in our oblivion of inner turmoil that it is almost impossible to appreciate life at hand.

I am myself living in the now as a single parent. I do sometimes dwell on past regrets and future concerns. Apart from making some necessary plans for the future, I try not to be too hung up on what's ahead. As for what is past, you can't change what was, so there's no gain in punishing yourself for things you wish you had done differently. My motto is this: Make the most of the present—my world as it is—and be grateful for all the wonderful moments that blend into my now. When my mind plucks me out of the present, which it often does, I try to anchor myself back in by focusing on my senses—on what I can see, touch, feel, and smell. I also become aware of my breathing. These things silence my mind, allowing me to reposition my awareness back to the moment. It is amazing what a calming effect this can have.

Personally, I don't want for much, that is, in the way of material things. I believe that the most important things in life are good health and happiness. I figure that, if you have these two assets throughout life, then you actually have everything you need.

People are often amazed at how happy people who live in Third World countries are. Material possessions are scant, yet these people are very much a happy community. Why is that? Is it because they find pleasure in the simple things in life? They often have a good family structure, with immediate and extended family members living together or at least nearby, which gives individual members a stronger sense of well-being and love. In Western society, we often get caught up in the stressors of life that come about as we work more to acquire all of the things we think we need or feel pressured into having. This chaos often creates stress. Too much stress can lead to illness, which can then lead to not having the time to enjoy those things we strive so hard for in the first place. We forget the basic human needs of love, food, safety, and shelter and go beyond, seeking fulfilment in other things we don't actually need. The simple things don't seem to be enough in our ever-evolving world, and insecurities stem from not being able to keep up appearances of fitting into the niche with everyone else.

In a world of materialism and instant gratification, keeping our children satisfied becomes more of a challenge, as does teaching them true values in life. What do you say or do when your child wants for more than he or she has in material possessions? There is a valid point in keeping up with other kids so your child feels on even keel, and keeping within the limits of affordability. There is also the question of what is really necessary, and what is fueled by desire. Where do you draw the line?

I think that it is important to tread carefully so as not to give in, give too soon, or give too much, at the same time keeping your child's self-esteem intact. You don't want your child to feel left out or as if he or she is lagging behind too often, as that will affect his or her self-worth. At the same time, you may have to make decisions according to finances available, and in a single-parent family you are often working with a smaller budget. I have had many a battle with my son regarding what he wants and what I can afford and what I feel he should wait to obtain. Going back to my own childhood, I remember feeling more of a thrill when I had to wait for a desired something, rather than being given it straight away. Delayed gratification teaches patience and appreciation— desired qualities to carry throughout life.

To forge through the battle of desiring more, I reinforce to my son the truth that there will always be someone better off and someone worse off than we are ourselves. As a child often takes things at face value, it's a good idea to expose your child to people who are less fortunate than you are. There are diversities among the people in our world—from those who are poverty stricken to those of countless riches. Apart from the need to feel secure, there is no evidence to suggest that financial status has anything to do with our level of happiness.

I have found that, despite the initial disappointment of discovering something my child desires that (in his words) "everyone else has," he will experience greater appreciation for that same thing when there is a substantial waiting period attached to his receiving it. It also goes beyond personal items. Not having ready finances has the advantage of giving us the appreciation of saving towards something. That something could be as simple as a weekend away or a small house renovation.

Instant gratification seems to be more likely the case in families of a high socio-economic status, when things can be obtained more readily. If circumstances change, it can be difficult to adjust to delayed gratification. Having to wait not only teaches patience, it can also determine a stronger character in preparation for life's unforeseen events.

A lot of us desire what we don't have—a better car, a bigger house, a house with a pool, siblings (when you don't have any), no siblings (when there's sibling rivalry), and on and on. My belief is that you can only ever live in the moment, so it's important to be grateful for what that moment presents. Your desires of obtaining something that you don't have, or a bigger or better something else, needn't interfere with your enjoyment of life. The chances are that you have had times in your life where you have had the pleasure of enjoying those same things you wish for, as life presented you that moment to do so. It really doesn't matter if you don't have ownership. All you need to do is take advantage of any and every moment that provides you the pleasure you desire.

My personal desire was to have a bigger family, to have more children to love and care for. When I look at my life, I realize I have had many moments that have equally fulfilled my desires. I've enjoyed many experiences with nieces and nephews and friends' children that have brought me wonderful pleasures and times spent with extended family members and friends as equally pleasurable. Might I add that some of those times spent have been in beautiful houses and at other lovely locations, none of which I can personally claim ownership of. It doesn't matter. I still get to live in the moment.

Whenever I envy something I don't have, I remind myself that I have plenty of moments now and ahead of me to simply enjoy many of life's joys—which are open and free to us all.

I firmly believe that, if a child is taught to have the same outlook—to enjoy the moments presented to him or her in life—then he or she can obtain true inner satisfaction . Children in a two-person household may often desire to live in a bigger family unit. If they can be taught to focus on the moments spent with extended family members and friends, they may learn that these times can just as well fill the void they think they are missing. In cases where there aren't any other family members around, good friends are just as good a substitute.

Fully experiencing each moment is truly rewarding. Being able to engage in and stay within the moment can take considerable effort sometimes, as our thoughts can interrupt our pleasure by dwelling on past regrets or future concerns. If we allow this to happen, our focus will be lost, and the moment will be gone. So put aside all other thoughts and enjoy what you are involved in—living in the now.

Once we're engaged in a certain activity the moment provides, we can become suspended in a state of subconsciousness, focused on our enjoyment, creating a sense of well-being. We are far away from all our troubles and cares, as our conscious mind is switched off. Of course that conscious mind can quickly come back into play as a result of any distractions. In our current world of advanced technology, our minds can easily be diverted by something simple yet demanding—the rings and vibrations of that little device we now carry on our bodies as though it were a necessary limb. Yes, you guessed it—I'm talking about the mobile phone! So if all your loved ones are accounted for and you aren't expecting an urgent call, switching off your mobile phone will help you remain in the moment and in the relaxed, serene, peaceful state that's been created.

We live in a world of cyber connections nowadays. You only have to look around you to observe people at a social gathering texting and updating the latest news on social media, totally oblivious to the moment they had made a special effort to attend and be involved in! Not only is this activity antisocial, the unnecessary interruption can have a rippling effect on all those involved in the enjoyment of the moment.

The simple pleasures in life are free. Yet the more materialistic and technical our world becomes, the harder it is to see the wood for the trees. We may need to train ourselves to be able to fully enjoy what we have in hand and to be grateful for what's really important.

Reminding ourselves to be appreciative of being in the moment can help keep us grounded, enhance our enjoyment, and add strength to our character.

Family Dynamics

There is no such thing as the perfect parent or the perfect child.

We all have our individual upbringings, experiences, conditioning, and temperaments that we subconsciously bring into our parenting styles. And then our children also have their individual grooming. So despite our best efforts or intentions, sometimes things just don't go as planned.

Consider this: You have had a good day and are on your way home. Your mood is upbeat, and you make plans to have a nice relaxing evening with your child, where you enjoy each other's company. Then something goes amiss. Your child is not in a similar mood. Far from it! Suddenly, what you had in mind dissipates. You not only feel disheartened, you now have to shift your mental state into a more fitting one for the occasion. Perhaps it is better that you are in a good mood rather than not to deal with it, or maybe this incident has changed your mood dramatically. Either way, you are faced with a predicament, one that either puts you into automatic pilot (when you act according to your conditioning before thinking) or manual gear (where you make a conscious effort to assess the situation before you act on it). Which is the best mode? Well the one in which you think before you act of course. It is, nevertheless, so much easier to react before you think! Much as it is when comparing driving an automatic geared car to a manual geared car.

So how do we deal with this? Just know that, whenever possible, it's best to stop and use your thinking brain. It is so easy to switch onto automatic pilot and react to the situation by yelling, ignoring, or abusing our children as we let our conditioning or temperaments get the better of us. As you already know, this will only have a negative effect on your child. And to boot, the situation may escalate, taking it further out of control.

By thinking before you react, you are more likely to remain calm and in control of the situation. Your child will also react in a more positive way in a nonthreatening environment. *Huh, so much easier said than done,* you may think, especially when you are a sole parent with no one else to back you up. Undoubtedly, parenting may be an easier road when another person is present to take on parental duties—when you can just step back when it gets a little too difficult or out of control. On the other hand, the other parent may not be present during the difficult situation, in which case it is out of his or her control. Or maybe the other parent is present but, according to his or her particular mood or individual conditioning, not on the same page as you, and so you don't get the support you need or want.

The onus is on you ultimately. Get it right as often as you can. And when you don't, there is no benefit in regrets. What I have personally found most helpful after turning off autopilot is sitting down with my child when the dust settles (when that frontal lobe of my brain has deactivated, and I go back to my conscious thinking brain) and talking it over. That conversation involves apologizing for my negative behaviour, explaining that I reacted without thinking. Then we talk about the event, carefully dissecting everything that was said in the heat of the moment. It is vital at this stage to make amends, to explain why you reacted the way you did. You want your child to understand human emotions, to put them into perspective. If the event is left unedited, there can be untoward negative consequences.

I always think on reflection, *What a waste of time that was losing my cool!* If only I had remained calm I would have saved time, by not needing to later put time and energy into rectifying the situation. Nevertheless, I will admit that, depending on my mood at the time, I am still a culprit of repeating the same track. To devise a positive from this, I can only hope that, through my many (and needless to say, repeated) explanations to my child, I am instilling in him a sense of right and wrong.

If a situation is left unresolved, then frustrations remain, and the next encounter may snowball into something much bigger than expected. Therefore, it is vital that you talk it over as soon as possible. The longer it is left unexplored, the greater the likelihood of creating lingering unhappiness and distress.

An only child in a two-person household has no one else to bounce ideas off or debrief with other than the parent. If a situation involves a disagreement, argument, or anything else that conjures up a negative emotion, the child has no one else to turn to and no siblings to make comparisons with. Without anyone to go to and vent or talk things over with, he or she may internalize things and carry a lot of blame.

I believe it is imperative to always find the time once tempers have played out, yet soon after a tense event, to calmly go over what happened so that your child doesn't carry any negativity or blame that, if left to accumulate, can affect his or her self-esteem. This is especially important when there follows a period of substantial separation from your child— for example, if the negative interaction occurs at bedtime or prior to school or childcare drop off. No matter what, you don't want your child to have a disturbed sleep, to experience lingering bad feelings, or to lack concentration in class. The longer a situation is left unresolved, the longer it has to fester and conjure up negative emotions. An argument is mostly always blown out of proportion. It is easy for an adult to see that on reflection, but a child hasn't yet the maturity to see it in the same way.

In the case of a young child when explanations won't suffice, as they won't always be understood, show your child that your love is unconditional by displaying lots of affection and spending extra special time together with him or her. By the way, that strategy works equally as well with children of all ages.

It is important that your child doesn't remain angry. To lighten things after a negative event, take some time to have a little fun or laughter to further diffuse the situation. The endorphin release will dissolve any remaining disharmony.

When it comes to temperaments, you and your child may be similar or at two different ends of the spectrum. If your temperaments are similar, parenting your child may be a lot easier than if the opposite is the case. We don't have a lot of control over our inherent temperaments. We just have to do our best to understand the differences and learn to deal with them as best we can.

As a single parent of an only child, I have become very aware of how isolated my child feels after we have been at loggerheads. I did consider getting him a dog so at least he would have someone to go to provide him some comfort, not to mention a loyal companion. That didn't eventuate, so I encouraged him to cuddle his soft toys whenever he felt alone. When he outgrew that, I allowed him an activity he could do to enable him to unwind and one which boosted his "feel-good" hormones. Such activities included; watching something fun on television, playing on his games console, or allowing him time to do something enjoyable like mess up the lounge room to build a fortress or create an obstacle course. Knowing that it is good to express all of the emotions, good and bad, I have encouraged my son to fully express each.

Anger can be a bit tricky, as people and things can be easy damaged during an outburst. And that has certainly been the case in our household from time to time. When tempers flare, it is difficult to act with a rational mind. In the interest of allowing the emotion to play out, I have encouraged certain actions that are non-threatening or harmful, such as bashing the beanbag and pillows and punching into the bed mattress and anything else that won't be damaged or cause damage to the person hitting them. I have found that finding a healthy way to experience and show anger, has to be instilled over and over again to become effective. Let's just say that the more it is enforced, the better the brain will remember it. Not that you can always expect the rational mind to always prevail. Indeed not. At least sometimes, it will provide a cushioning affect.

In a two-parent household, you have the advantage of swapping out from the driver's seat when you feel exhausted or at your wits' end. Then the other parent can direct the course. After all, your co-parent has an equal interest in the care and responsibility of your child. Even if you have dealt with a situation on your own, you can later discuss it with the other parent when he or she returns home (or even over the telephone if you are separated and on amicable terms).

As an only parent, with no other parent present or available as backup, it is up to you to manage the best way possible. There may be times when you just want to throw in the towel, particular days on which you just don't want to parent. When you are having a day like that, it may be helpful to take a step back and call a well-trusted family member or friend. That person may be able to help you put things into perspective. With support, you may find other tools to work with and the encouragement you need to soldier on. Sometimes you just need a listening ear, someone to whom you can vent. If you are lacking in a social network, then there are parent helplines available.

Removing yourself from an unsavoury situation will temporarily give yourself and your child some breathing space. This can be very difficult to do, and I am not implying that I always manage to do so. I don't. I do, however, think that it is very necessary to make a sustained effort, considering the fact that your child has no one else to go to.

Even though you may be raging inside, time out will simmer your anger and that of your child. Although stepping away from a heated situation requires considerable effort, each time you do it, you will find it becomes more manageable.

There will be those times when you feel that a confrontation is your fault—that you instigated the whole situation, which quickly became out of hand, because you had a rough day, were in a bad mood, or were frustrated over other stressors in life. You'll want to make peace because, underneath, you'll be feeling guilty for being out of line. Instead of feeling guilty, we are better off acknowledging our mistakes and reconciling. That way, when we act before we think (on autopilot) and say things we later regret, apologizing will not only help put things into perspective and ease tensions, it will also provide a valuable lesson for our children. If they see us acting in such a way, they will be more likely to emulate our behaviour.

There will be times when your child is in a "mood" and may have an unexpected outburst. If we focus on the child's behaviour without delving into the mental process that defines the behaviour, we miss the opportunity of allowing him or her to learn about the complex issues that influence human behaviour. Look at what may be behind the mood—perhaps tiredness, a bad day at school, bullying, a fight with a friend, or whatever else may have been the cause of distress. Often, we are so involved in our own stressors in life that we forget our children are also at the mercy of stress. Demonstrating empathy and acting accordingly, rather than reacting to the mood with negative emotion, will allow our child to see and understand that it is okay to have ups and downs.

We can assist in the development of future insight in our children. By later discussing the core of the matter, we will help them develop their character and enable them to handle future social interactions. Our children will come to understand that there are transient shifts in all peoples' moods, not just their own, and that these states of mind ebb and flow according to thought processes in the moment. And engaging in post-reflection on the cause of a particular mood or a relationship fracture will provide insight that will help children tolerate those overblown, out-of-hand ruptures that sometimes occur in families.

It is within our parental nature to want to protect our children, and we may go to great lengths to do that. We want to shield them from the many hurts and discomforts in life, as seeing them hurt and upset can be heart-wrenching.

The only child can intensify this need, as this child is our only immediate family—our one focus. In fact, it is difficult to know when to step aside and allow your child independence and autonomy. I have found that it is all too easy to carry on doing things for my son, much of which he could do himself if I'd have just left him to it. I'm referring to physical things, such as washing, ironing, and putting away his clothes, preparing all his meals, packing his bag, and so on. (These things I am still working on!) On a psychological level, I try to make an effort to allow him to fend for himself and tackle his own battles. Mistakes and bad days are a part of life, and as much as we want to cushion our children from them and keep them in happy mode, we need to allow them to experience the pain, tears, embarrassment, and consequences of their own mistakes and the disappointments of a less than good day. They need to learn to develop their own skills for dealing with what life throws at them. Standing aside yet readily available, we as parents can still be their safety net. Our children need to know that they can come to us to discuss situations and that we will help them make decisions. We, the older, wiser ones, can make suggestions and reinforce that there is always a positive lesson to be learnt from mistakes made and those days that just don't go our way.

The display of unhappy emotions can too easily lead you to rescue your child from the cause of upset, especially when you want to immediately sooth him or her. Perhaps you can't bear your child's hurt, or maybe he or she is becoming annoying and you have neither the patience nor the time to deal with it. Perhaps it may be that you jump in too quickly when you don't have the support of another parent or reasonable adult to confer with. A quick fix may rectify the negative emotion. However, it has the potential to cripple your child's emotional development. So putting in the hard yards of perseverance is well worth every effort. Remember to treat yourself for your tremendous work!

· · · · · · · · · ● · · · · · · · · · ·

Hug It Out

If anger or frustration is taking too long to defuse, hug it out, even when you least feel like it! I can't claim this as being my own idea; it came from a single mother of three boys. My good friend and colleague suggested that I do this, so I put it into practice. Swearing under my breath, I would take my son into my arms to hug it out. Stiffened bodies soon become supple (be patient it may take a few minutes) as the hug softens. Words needn't be exchanged as each feels that love remains intact.

Tactile expression reinforces love, warmth, and security. Isn't that what we all want and need regardless of our age? A hug, cuddle, or touch activates our feel-good hormones—serotonin and endorphins. A hug can transform a mood in an instant. Touch is one of our basic senses and is first experienced straight after birth when a mother cradles her infant. In fact, there is a surge of powerful hormones in both mother and child just prior to birth, instigating bonding. And an ongoing secretion of hormones maintains and strengthens connections. Physical closeness continues to be a fundamental human need throughout life.

* * * * * * * * * ● * * * * * * * * *

Keeping the Peace

Wouldn't it be great sometimes to have another adult person living with you—someone to offload your troubles to and to give you some tender, loving care when you most need it? Equally as important, you'd have someone to pull you in line when you have overstepped the boundaries. Being out of bounds probably happens more often than you are aware of, simply because there's no one to point it out—well at least no other mature adult. Your child may question or arc up at your behaviour, though you take this as "giving cheek" or being disrespectful. In the moment, you're not able to stand aside and see things as they truly are, and the situation may escalate way further than expected.

You may be well aware that you aren't in the best of moods because you are tired, stressed, upset over an incident that happened at work (or some other place outside of home), or simply just fed up with things. Your child inadvertently becomes your scapegoat, because he or she is the only other human being at home to dump on. It's not as though you can come home and offload on anyone else. (Well, you could maybe use the cat or the dog if you have one!) There are times you need to talk things over with another person, to debrief whatever happened during the day. Another adult would be ideal, although that's not an option. You are the only grown up in the household. You're in a mood; you take it out on your child. You know you shouldn't; it just sometimes happens. You are in a state of autopilot. The conscious mind is temporarily suppressed, and without intent, the brunt of your mood taints your child.

We don't have anyone else around to give us a nudge, to tell us that we are being unreasonable—at least not anyone with adult maturity. Our child might be desperately trying to tell us! If we had a mediator comment, "Hey, you're being a bit harsh on the kid," we could possibly switch back to the rational mind more readily, and our dear child may be saved from wearing more of our mood than was ever intended.

So what do we do about this? I think an understanding that this can be a common occurrence is the first thing. Awareness may stop you in your tracks sometimes, before the situation gets out of hand. In the event that you have gone too far, then the best thing to do is to explain this to your child. Apologize to him or her, ensuring the child understands that it has all come about as a result of your own frustrations so that he or she doesn't carry any blame.

A child may think that adults know everything and have everything under control—that as an adult you can contain emotions and that there is nothing more left for you to learn. Of course, children are growing and maturing so their level of understanding is different at various stages. Your awareness of this and ability to handle the situation accordingly will enhance your child's acceptance of your apology.

Our ability to tell our children how we are feeling and that our negative emotion has nothing to do with them helps them put things in perspective. If your child is too young to hear an explanation, then giving him or her plenty of kisses, cuddles, and undivided attention will dissipate feelings of helplessness. When we aren't emotionally available, another adult can suffice in giving the approval and affection our child requires. This can come from other family members, friends, or even neighbours—anyone with whom the child has a trusting relationship. Later on, when we are feeling more normal, we should then make a conscious effort to spend quality time with our child to make up for the distance and perhaps confusion created earlier.

What may add to our temper and frustration is that we are doing it all on our own. We don't have the advantage of a partner's words of encouragement. We never hear the words we often long for: "You're doing a great job." "Put your feet up. Let me take something on." "Don't worry about this. Things will work out." We have to give ourselves that pat on the back.

So do so! Tally up the tough times and make a note to spoil yourself in some way. It could be something as simple as treating yourself to a glass of wine or that block of chocolate you have stashed away or whatever else takes your fancy. Whenever possible, allow yourself a bigger treat if you can manage it. Needless to say, it is best not to overindulge in unhealthy treats, as the consequences could outweigh the benefits! But if you do, so what? Accept that you are human and, as such, not perfect; there will be times when your behaviour will be less than desired. Whenever you drift off the rails, just know that you are more than capable of rectifying the situation. Remain positive!

We all have a need to be taken care of emotionally, and in a household with only one adult—you—allow yourself to do the honours. Your psychological well-being is just as important as you physical well-being. And so is that of your child's. There's no point in persevering with something if your frustrations are mounting, or if you are too tired or just not in the right frame of mind. Take a break. If you are able, arrange some childcare so you can get out of the house for a while. If that's impossible, call someone close to you with whom you can have a chat. In any case, stepping away from a situation that has the potential of getting out of hand, even if just for a few minutes, will allow you to gather your rational thoughts, even if they are a little slow at seeping back in. It will also give your child some time out, something a child is unequipped to initiate for him or herself.

How easy is it sometimes to give in in order to keep the peace? I have been able to vouch for that on more than a few occasions. I find it occurs more often when I'm tired, stressed, or generally unwell. Giving in is an easy way out. Your child wants something: "Can l have …?" Your answer is a *firm no* to start with. Before too long, it becomes a *not-so-firm no*, eventually dissipating to a *maybe* and preceding rapidly to a total surrender—*all right then, just have it!*

I think we all know what's best—sticking to that firm no in the beginning without any deviation! Doing so, however, takes perseverance, which requires energy we don't always have. We just want some peace, so to acquire that (our most pressing need), we give in to our child's demands. That way, we can get on with nursing that headache or emotional hurt or purely indulging in our own desires. Unfortunately, if we give in too readily, our child learns how to play our buttons, which can then turn into manipulative behaviour.

So we need to muster up some energy somehow in a moment we least feel like doing so. A lot of the time, our children will sense our mood or at least our distancing from them and be more demanding in an attempt to gain some attention. We in turn, so involved in our own selves, don't always pick up on this and push our child away. Feeling disregarded and hurt, our child steps in to "pester" us even more! Soon enough, all hell breaks loose. As soon as one of our red buttons is activated, many more come in to play—like a domino effect we can't easily stop.

Wouldn't it have been more peaceful in the long run if we had given the time to have dealt with our child's demands in the beginning? It is well worth providing the energy required then and there because, if a situation gets out of hand, we then have to conjure up more energy. And that's precisely what we intended to avoid in the beginning! Before too long, we could be drawing on an empty reserve tank. Also, if our child feels as though he or she has secured an adequate amount of attention to begin with, then he or she will be happier and less likely to be demanding, and so it becomes a win-win scenario.

Television, computer games, and other technical devices have the advantage of keeping our children occupied and less likely to be of an annoyance to us, especially when we want some time out or are in need of getting something done. This can be a good thing when we need that break, but we do have to be responsible parents and put limits on those activities. Even though these devices can create entertainment and peace, prolonged use can dampen creativity, instigate addiction, and take away precious family togetherness.

* * * * * * * * ● ● ● ● ● ● ● ● * * * *

Death of the Xbox

It was a Saturday morning when the Xbox died. It wasn't that my son spent every waking moment on his console, but his free time had lately been consumed by the entertainment it provided. Not to mention the moments of uninterrupted peace it provided me over the weekend, enabling me to get things done—namely some writing!

After much time spent, or should I say wasted, on sorting out a remedy—that being when the Xbox could be replaced (and with the newest version)—my son discovered some new talents. As I have discussed, I believe in delayed gratification. However, I was very tempted to cash in some savings on instant gratification and replace the Xbox immediately—when my child became an annoyance to me. Needless to say, he was disappointed that there was a sudden interruption to his gaming pleasure. He became panicked and wanted an instant fix. The nagging commenced, and he filled me in on what others have that he doesn't. He was "getting in my hair" with his far-too-often expressed notion that he had "nothing else to do."

He did, as it turned out, find something else to do and opened up a creative side of himself. He busied himself posting an informative YouTube video (yes, this new outlet still involved technology) and playing his guitar. I was able to take a sigh of relief and get back to some "me time." More importantly, I noticed how my child's mood changed; he was happier experiencing some personal satisfaction.

Eventually, the Xbox was replaced. I constantly find that I have to make a conscious effort to police the time my son spends on gaming. It's all too easy to lose track of time and not care about it when I am completely involved in my own projects. In fact, I have to pull myself back from allowing him more time when it's really more of my own time that I desire.

* * * * * * * ● ● ● ● ● ● ● * * * *

PART 2

Perseverance

Questions Raised

Apart from the traditional questions on origins and family history, there may be some tricky questions to deal with in the two-person household. Each of us has unique circumstances and, as such, questions may vary. Here I will talk about how I dealt with questions raised pertaining to my own circumstances, and hopefully this may be of some benefit to you as well.

Above all else post-separation, what to tell my child was my main concern. I thought I would have time to think this through. Then the first question presented itself: "Where's Daddy?" My child had just turned two.

I had asked the counsellor what I should tell my son, how I should explain things according to his maturity. I didn't get an answer in black and white so to speak, so I dealt with the questions as they arose. I found that honesty always prevailed. Of course, you have to choose answers based on the age of your child. A little information at first can be expanded on later.

What I found particularly helpful was anticipating the probable questions so that I could formulate answers to them ahead of time. That way, I felt more prepared to deal with any of those curve balls thrown my way.

Following, "where's daddy?" here are some of the other questions my son asked me:

- "Why don't I have a father?" (four years of age)
- "I had two dads, and now I don't have any. Why? I'm a good boy." (six years of age following the breakup of a subsequent relationship)

- "Why did you leave Dad?" (eight years of age)
- "Can't you and Dad work things out and get back together?" (nine years of age)
- "Why did you pick the wrong person to marry?" (eleven or twelve years of age)

These were some of the questions my son voiced. I am sure there were others he kept to himself. By maintaining a gentle, honest approach I found these questions easier to answer than I had anticipated. Even though it was sometimes heartbreaking to have to deal with these questions, I always felt better after each of them were answered and with as much information as possible. Issues were discussed according to my son's maturity at the time. When my child was out of character; quiet, sulky or despondent, I intuitively felt the need to probe a little, revealing some of those unvoiced questions and we dealt with those as well.

So what did I tell my child? How did I answer the questions? I tried to take the diplomatic approach. Sometimes I was able to think my answers through, and at other times questions took me by surprise, and I would have to think up answers on the spot. When l thought an answer wasn't understood or wasn't the answer l would have given had l had time to think about it, l would readdress it later. My gut feeling would tell me whether or not my child felt satisfied with the answers l gave him.

I believed I needed to be open and frank with the answers I gave, sugarcoating things when I needed to without being dishonest. Acknowledging and addressing feelings as they surfaced helped take the bite out of a difficult emotion, for both myself and my child.

As we are our children's primary guides and protectors, we owe it to them to be as honest as possible. We do want them to know that they can come to us for anything and that they can trust us to tell them the truth.

I am in no way implying that I explained everything well or in as much detail as I could have at times. My son repeated some of these questions at various ages, so I had the opportunity to go over aspects of the answers that, perhaps, he didn't fully understand at a younger age. I did employ the help of a child psychologist, for the personal benefit of my child and to assist me with some strategies.

I did learn through close friends and the child psychologist that there were, indeed, questions my son didn't ask me, even from a very young age—questions he felt were too delicate to ask his mother. I wasn't aware of this at all. My son and I have always had a close relationship, and I thought he would ask me anything there was to ask. I would regularly probe him for anything more and often thought that the slate was clean after our discussions. When I was informed of some of the questions he'd voiced to another trusted person, I felt I had failed him.

I have come to acknowledge that your child won't always tell you everything; there will be lingering unasked questions, things left unsaid. Knowing this is a great asset, as you can direct your child to another person in whom he or she trusts to discuss matters. It's not a matter of obtaining particular information for yourself rather than resolving issues for your child. Finding someone for your child to talk to about things he or she may not feel comfortable discussing with you, as his or her parent, allows your child an avenue to air certain matters. During such discussions, there may be some important issues revealed that require further attention, and you should trust that same person to tell you of such so that you can seek further assistance for your child if needs be. Some things, though, just need to be aired. If a trusted person provides that listening ear and understanding and your child feels resolution, then so be it.

For those questions that remain unasked—and I'm assuming there are probably a few—I try to guess the subject matter and offer some relevant information. It's a stab in the dark I know, but it's worth a try. I sometimes think I hit the bullseye or at least get close enough to it!

We all have our own beliefs about our existence and what happens when we depart this life. Without discrediting your beliefs in any way, I would like to share mine.

I believe in a greater power. Raised as a Catholic, I believe in God and a life after death. Yet I don't believe that this is our only life. I think we have many lessons to learn, and we are reincarnated into different lives to complete these lessons. Once our life journeys are complete, we then enter the afterlife as a spiritual being in an existence eternally with God.

This belief has helped me answer the questions my son has raised. Without the intention of brainwashing him, I have explained my beliefs to him. I have told him that this is just one of his lives, and that, in between lives, he is given a choice of what life to live next and a snippet preview of that life. In that preview, a picture is revealed of his future life, and he then decides whether to take on that life or choose another. I have pointed out that he must have seen some good aspects in his life to have chosen the one he did. I also reinforce the positives in his life—a close extended family, good friends, and opportunities to look forward to that present themselves continuously throughout life.

No one knows what's around the corner in life, which door will open next. Life always includes an element of surprise. We can't look into the future, and just as well, as then we may very well get bored. Whenever my child feels that life is unfair or that he is missing out in any way, I point this out, adding that answers to our questions often appear as life unfolds.

There have been times when my child has grieved the loss of his father's presence in his life and times that he has wished for siblings. That is, of course, normal, and grief should be expressed. What I have done during these times is empathize with him, so that he knows I understand his despair, and shower him with my love. I reinforce that there are many different family structures, all of them considered normal in our society. In the case of our own family, we are just two in a house, yet we have close relationships with many other (extended) family members. We also have very close family friends who we consider just as important in our lives. So it doesn't matter that we don't all live under the same roof. We still get to spend quality time with the people we love as often as we can.

Intuition comes from an inner feeling, somewhere deep within. Some people may describe it as our spiritual guidance. Sometimes we can't find the right answers no matter how hard we search. We just have to rely on our inklings. If we trust in and act on our instincts, we usually find answers we so desperately need, particularly at those times, when we are otherwise overcome with panic and uncertainty, and all other answers seem obscure.

Time Spent Together

I believe in devoting as much time as possible to your child, especially in a two-person household. You and your child need to establish and maintain a strong, loving, trusting, and enjoyable relationship, and for this to happen, it is important that you spend time together. This will involve doing activities together, as well as just being present in each other's company.

It is imperative that you form a strong bond with your only immediate family member. When there are other family members who live in the same household, then various other bonds will occur. When it's you and your child, only one bond can occur, and the best one would be one that is secured by love and trust.

We need to spend time together to feel loved and appreciated. We also need some time apart to consolidate those feelings. When our children are young, we spend most of our waking hours with them. As they grow and mature the apron strings loosen. And as they develop more and more independence, they break away from our ties. So it's important to have a good relationship with our children before those apron strings are completely severed. We want to develop lasting relationships and not slacken off just because we feel our child is more independent and doesn't need us as much.

When I became a single parent, l wanted to create and maintain a stable environment for my family. Whenever l was away from my child, as l juggled work and family life, l needed him to feel secure. Even though l had numerous offers of help with childcare, l chose those people who my child was closest to and most comfortable with. I tried to restrict his caregivers to a select few in order to develop a sense of continuity. By not being shuffled around between too many caregivers, my child would, I hoped, feel secure.

I felt it important to reduce my work hours as much as possible during my son's preschool and primary school years. I wanted to spend as much time with him as possible. Understandably, you may not be in a position to free up time. You just need to make the most of the time you have. Those primitive years are vital in directing developmental milestones that lay down the foundations of your child's personality, demeanour, and disposition, all of which will determine how he or she responds to the world.

Time together perpetuates feelings of being well cared for, loved, and valued. Children are more likely to grow up to be confident, happy, and well-adjusted members of society if they spend a good amount of time with their parent(s) or guardian(s).

Looking after a young child involves a lot of supervision and general care, so there is a lot of time spent together. Apart from caring for a young child being hard work, children are very cute and cuddly at this age, which can make time spent together very enjoyable. Their cuteness fades as they become older. And during the pre-teen and teenage stage, as they seek autonomy, they can become quite difficult to spend time with.

Despite a child's age, he or she does require frequent periods of your undivided attention, for healthy psychological development. Being available to watch your children participate in sports or other activities that are important to them demonstrates your interest. Creating special time together—where you are wholly involved in an activity that is of interest to your child—will strengthen your relationship. Our love and support is reflected in the gifts of time we give our children.

How often are we involved in the mundane chores of life when our child instantaneously requires our attention? What do we do? Often we tell them to wait because we are busy reading the paper, doing the dishes, cleaning the house, ironing, or whatever else (things that could easily be put on hold). It may not even be a physical chore that they are interrupting; it could be that we are busy in our heads with mind chatter, sorting out concerns. Wouldn't it be better to stop what we are doing or thinking for the time being and soak in the spontaneity of the moment, before it becomes completely lost? Not only that, each time we tell our children we are too busy, we add a little deflation to their ego.

As difficult as it sometimes is to stop something midstream and devote ourselves to listening to or observing our child, it is important to do so. If your child is subject to the "not now" or "wait, I'm busy" responses too often, he or she may be less inclined to come to you to show or discuss something with you. Your child doesn't have the advantage of seeking out another person in the house when you're not available, so the lack of attention or rejection he or she feels is magnified.

Although they may appear quite self-sufficient, teenagers require a good deal of our attention. Emotions are turbulent as independence and identity emerge. Having a conversation with your teen can be difficult enough, let alone finding an activity the two of you can share! If it's difficult to come up with something to share in together, just being present, close by, and available will keep the channels of communication open.

Teenagers are often preoccupied as they develop a sense of their own identity and where they fit in in the world. It is important to be available to guide teens through this delicate process. At the same time, it is also important to respect their need for privacy. A teen's brain nerve cells are still forming essential layers necessary for adequate transmission of information. An understanding of the immaturity of the teenage brain should enable us to comfortably step aside at times and let things be. We shouldn't feel offended when we are pushed away. We and our teenagers are on two different spectrums after all, and it doesn't take much to recall our own feelings and disposition when we were once teens!

• • • • • • • • ● ● ● ● • • • • • • • •

Brick Walls

Do you ever find it impossible to talk to your teen? You want to spend quality time together, yet he or she wants to spend time in his or her room or doing something else. You feel disappointed. After all, you were looking forward to this time in your lives that you could do things together and have interesting conversations. Or so you hoped! Maybe you need to have an important discussion about things, and it's just not the right time. So you decide to put it off until tomorrow. Tomorrow comes, you get busy, forget, or the timing is off once again. You don't want to leave it, especially as you are the sole parent/family member. This is the time to be thankful for mobile phones. You can be assured that your teenager will read a text or e-mail. Your message could contain something depicting how important your teen is to you, and you may even book a suitable time to spend together or have that discussion. This will demonstrate that you care and are very much a presence in your child's life, albeit sometimes a silent one.

• • • • • • • • ● ● ● ● • • • • • • • •

It can be difficult to allow teenagers as much alone time as they require when you are a single parent, as you then have to deal with your own feelings of isolation. Your sweet child, who not long ago spent time cuddling up to you on the couch whilst you both enjoyed a television program or movie, becomes confined to the privacy of his or her own bedroom, emerging only at meal times or to get a snack. You start to communicate in the house via text messages!

You may crave the company of your child in an otherwise empty house. Your child, on the other hand, desperately seeks autonomy. I think that accepting that this is the normal, healthy progression of the maturing teenager and not in any way a reflection on whether or not your teen enjoys spending time with you helps put things in perspective.

Although at times it can be hard to find a happy medium, you should still find activities to share and time to spend together. Even if the activity you settle on is something you don't particularly like to do, remember that the sole purpose of the activity is to share in each other's company, and in participating, you will reinforce a close, healthy bond between you and your child.

During the teenage years, there are plenty of hours of togetherness clocked up in the car. Take advantage of those car trips, taxi servicing your teen. It is often a good time to talk, joke, or generally enjoy each other's company.

Car trips can be the perfect opportunity to have important discussions. There are often times I need to talk to my son about important issues, and when a subject enters my head, it's not always an appropriate time to have that conversation. I postpone the discussion to a more suitable time, which can be whilst on a car journey, the longer the better. Just think, there are no distractions and no trying to run away. So as not to forget, I make a mental note to myself or even jot it down somewhere, as there have been times that I have forgotten and missed good opportunities.

Part of your child feeling loved, cared for, and valued is dependent on your presence in his or her life. So even when your child develops more independence as a teenager, it is still very important to be around most of the time. As tempting as it may be to skip out of the house more often and for longer periods, your being a presence at home as much as you can be is comforting and reassuring to your child.

If a child feels undervalued because you aren't around often enough, communication can break down, and personality traits may deviate from those desired. The child may engage in unfavourable behaviour in order to seek attention or feel worthy. The time and effort applied to rectify this behaviour inevitably takes up a whole lot more energy than would have been necessary if time had been invested wisely initially.

Home Alone

I have to admit that, as soon as my son gained sufficient independence, I took advantage of the ability to go out, leaving him at home alone. After all, it was pretty easy. He did his own thing; I did mine. I was only a phone call away. As I sometimes work a few hours on weekends and weeknights, I was already conscious of him spending periods of time alone at home and tried to make an effort to not be gone too long during my social outings. I have left him for longer periods of time than what I initially intended.

Thinking back on my own childhood, I can still recall the emptiness I felt when home alone for a lengthy period of time. That feeling continued throughout adolescence and early adulthood. Despite my age, to this day, I still feel a pang of disappointment if I surprise visit my mother and she isn't home.

Even though you may be in separate rooms of the house, the presence of another, particularly a loved one, is very comforting. Just the simple sounds of the clattering of dishes in the kitchen, is evidence that there is someone else home, reassuring you that you are not alone.

When I felt that I was overdoing it and was consumed by feelings of guilt, sure I was neglecting my child, I pulled myself up and had a chat with my son. I explained that I thought him independent and that, for this reason, I had taken advantage of the situation, skipping out of the house. I reinforced that he is the most important thing to me and that, from then on, I would be more watchful of the time and frequency of my outings.

Actions speak louder than words as you already know, and as much as I want to stick to my word, I don't always. So when I am a culprit of staying away too long, I make an effort to immediately give my child undivided attention or, better yet, do something fun with him when I return. You could say I am squashing feelings of guilt. Yes, that's partly true. Another part of the equation, I hope, is that I'm reconnecting with my son on an emotional level so that the love bank remains on even kilter.

Creating family memories is a part of connectedness, and something that can be favourably drawn on in future years to come. We recall our memories better if they are associated with a strong emotional attachment, so special moments of fun and togetherness will sit well in our child's memory bank. Fond memories can be established when we set aside special family time, where we purposely participate in activities that become family tradition. This could be a regular weekend away, a holiday, or something as simple as a game night or a movie night.

Apart from an occasional weekend away, my son and I share traditions as simple as shooting baskets on an indoor basketball hoop after dinner on a Sunday night. If I forget or try and wriggle my way out of it, my son is quick to remind me: "Ah, come on, Mum. It's family tradition." I must admit, it does provide us with fun and laughter, which in turn triggers the release of endorphins, helpful to initiate a sense of relaxation and well-being.

It is important to me that my son be often exposed to the love, affection, and comradeship of his extended family so as to feel part of a bigger picture and develop another set of special memories. Close friends can be just as influential.

As much as we love our children and they us, we also need to spend time apart. Let's face it; we all become irritated by one another, even in the best of relationships, and we can irritate our children just as much as they can us at times. So we do need breaks from one another.

Parenting can be draining, as it is often a "give-give" relationship. The parent gives; the child takes. This is, of course, what we sign up for and expect as a parent. Yet if we aren't involved in a close relationship with a partner who can make some deposits into our love bank, then all we are left with are constant withdrawals from our child.

We have to look after ourselves so we can be better parents. We also need some respite from our children. Taking breaks from parenting enables us to come back fresh and rebooted. Feeling peaceful and content with our lives will reflect in our moods. We want to feel happy and upbeat and avoid the irritability and mood swings that can occur when we are exhausted. These breaks are very necessary and probably required on a more regular basis than if you were a fit of a bigger family, where other members can share in the demands of family life.

Often accompanied by taking time out is a feeling of guilt—guilt that you should be at home completing chores or that you need to spend more time with your child, rather than taking time out for yourself. Look at it this way: If you don't take the time out, you may be at home yet not readily available to your child, as frustrations based on your need for time out mount. On the other hand, if you do take time out and leave the house, you get to spend time away from your child and come back feeling re-energized and emotionally ready to give to your child when you return.

When my child was a preschooler, I put him into childcare one day a week just for time to myself. I did also reason that interaction with other children would be conducive to his development. I felt a bit mean at times when my child would plead with me to pick him up early and I would refuse to comply, as I needed "my time." I thought he was just being clingy. (I later learnt that he wasn't happy, as the childcare worker often shouted at the children. Whoops, another lesson learnt from not being a perfect parent.) As my child got older, I took advantage of play dates. I have been lucky to have family and friends help out as well, although I would mostly reserve their childcare services for the times that I worked. I often felt uncomfortable asking them to help out for other times, as I worried I may have been taking up too much of their time.

I believe that, as a single parent, you do rely on others to help you and you can sometimes feel that, by asking family and friends for assistance too frequently, you are overdoing it or maybe putting them out. To overcome this, look for ways in which you can help the person who helped you. Perhaps you can give some of your time, assisting your helper with a certain chore or project. Or maybe you can exchange return favours, such as child minding or car transporting. Or you might simply give appreciative gifts. You don't need to return favours straight away, especially when you are time poor. Keep a mental record of the good deeds done for you and give back when you can.

People do genuinely want to help out, and most don't expect anything in return, as being able to give to and help another human being is highly rewarding. On the other hand, we instinctively want to give back and feel awkward when we can't. Giving back can be as simple as showing our sincere appreciation. We know ourselves how satisfying it feels to give to another and that an acknowledgement of gratitude is all that we desire.

You and your child might be able to enjoy needed time apart from one another even when you are in the same surroundings. For example, a family or social gathering might be the perfect time. The dynamics change when you're both individually occupied by other people's company. You remain close by and, at the same time, perfectly distanced.

Too close a bond between parent and child, one in which there is limited or virtually no time apart, can have a restricting effect on the child developing his or her own sense of identity. Children need to explore the world in their own way, to encounter what life throws at them so as to devise their own coping strategies. If you don't allow your child the time and space to venture out into the world and spend time alone or at least independently of you, he or she won't discover his or her capabilities.

* * * * * * * * ● ●● * * * * * * * *

Memories

Even though I lived in a house that was falling away at the seams, there was plenty of love there! As a child, I fantasized about a two-storey house with a pool. My son does the same, although you can add a theatre room to his vision of the perfect house.

I recently spent some time delivering pamphlets. I felt a sense of nostalgia when passing by houses that looked like mine when I was growing up—those with the fallen letter boxes, peeling paint, and broken fences. They reminded me of my home and all the warm feelings attached to it.

Memories—it doesn't matter if they are created in a mansion or a shoebox—as long as they are laced with lots of love.

* * * * * * * * ● ●● * * * * * * * *

Networking: Create Your Community

People in business are often networking to create opportunities that mutually benefit one another in their respective professions. Social networking involves creating a network of social interactions and personal relationships, and like in business, these networks are also of mutual benefit.

Social networking can assist in reducing our workload and stress levels as we develop connections with people we can form bonds with. In doing so, we diminish feelings of isolation and build a network of people who socialize together and generally help each other out when help is required.

Networking can involve being in and maintaining close relations with extended family and friends, as well as creating new associations. Even if your partner is no longer around you, family-in-laws can still very much be a part of your lives. The bigger the network of people you have around you, the better.

You may have to choose a place to live so that you can be close to loved ones who can support you, although you can always make up your own community. Social media makes it very easy to find associated links to particular community services or groups that may be of interest to you. As I have previously mentioned, a single parents group can be a fabulous outlet, particularly during your child's preschool days when you are more homebound and not as exposed to the wider community as you will be when your child begins his or her school years.

Building a network involving existing friends, family members, and neighbours, including associations through groups formed and new friends, will enhance your well-being. Belonging to a community of people is uplifting, especially during times you feel alone and emotionally drained. Times shared with others often lighten our load, as we have others to share in our pleasures and help lift the burden of our troubles. We also have an array of people to call upon should we require childcare or any other support.

Make a list of anyone you could form stronger ties with—brothers, sisters, aunties, uncles, grandparents, nieces, nephews, cousins, or anyone else who comes to mind. Extending your family as much as possible will be of benefit to you and your child. You can then look outside your small immediate family and feel a larger part of the extended family, with all the trimmings included.

In a wider community, many role models will be available to your child. Exposure to people with admirable qualities and good moral values is important in your child's upbringing. Those assets can come from extended family members or from anyone else you befriend. As you are the only adult at home to emulate, you really do need to make a sustained effort throughout your child's growing years to manifest as many opportunities as possible to expose your child to suitable role models.

As my child is of the opposite sex from me, I expose him to as many male role models as possible. Luckily, our extended family members are predominately male, among them my son's cousins, who are young adults. Although they all live in different states, we make the most of family time spent together, even if it means my son stays up well over curfew. I want him to soak in all the maleness he can get.

There has never been a shortage of female role models in my son's life, so I feel confident that he has good exposure in that arena. I have, on the other hand, felt the need to up his male exposure whenever possible. Throughout my son's primary school years, only one male teacher was available, so I requested that my son be enlisted in that teacher's fourth grade class. One of the reasons I enrolled my child in karate was that I wanted him to gain some discipline from a male instructor. From then on, he has had male sports coaches and has been mentored and supported by other children's fathers at his games.

Time moves forward, and circumstances change. Your network may collapse in part or whole. Sometimes you need to start over or at least replace some people with others. Take every opportunity to rebuild or reinforce your support system. Make new friends and acquaintances through people you meet at childcare, kindergarten, schools, and sports or social events. Join a book group, community walking group, gymnasium, yoga class, or something else of interest to you.

People may assume you are coping well or are self-sufficient if you don't request offers of help or if you decline them. We are meant to help each other. The desire to assist others is a part of the innate nature within each of us. Yes, some people do appear to be more willing to lend a hand. However, it could just be that some people have more time on their hands than others or can read you well. Some people simply don't think to offer. If you appear to be managing, then people will assume you are, in deed, managing. Typically, those people with a well-developed empathy can see behind the scenes, and they are the ones who will be more likely to offer their services to you.

Often we are reluctant to ask for help, as we're afraid we may be infringing on another person's already busy life or cutting into his or her rare recreational time. Sometimes we decline offers of help for the same reasons or out of fear of appearing disorganized or incapable. We need to let go of our pride and accept that we do require help from others in all aspects of life. If that seems difficult, all we need do is recall the many times we have helped others. Requesting and accepting offers of help will free up valuable time, which we can spend with our most prized possessions—our children.

In modern Western cultures, the family unit usually consists of only the immediate family members living together. Children leave home when they are grown to establish their own dwellings, and the elderly are often later cared for in nursing homes. In other cultures, immediate and extended families live together or at least in the same vicinity. This enables sharing of workloads, savings in living costs, and closer family bonds, all of which contribute to diminished stress levels. There are also many hands on deck to take care of individual needs, especially useful when it comes to the young and elderly, who are the most dependant members. Care is shared, which takes the pressure off just one or two people doing it all.

Those of us who don't live in an extended family setup can at least simulate something close to it. We are capable of creating a support system, one that is of benefit to both ourselves and the people with whom we build it. We can perhaps share in caring for each other's children or do each other favours, either pertaining to the children or of a different nature.

Childcare can be expensive and difficult to afford when you have a limited income. My way around this was to employ a reputable older person who had plenty of time and a love of children and offer this person a basic acceptable amount of money to take care of my child. I managed to find two retirees. These women had grown families and no grandchildren. The benefits were twofold; I had the help that I required, and these women had the opportunity of filling in their spare time enjoying the pleasures of a young child. As soon as possible, starting when your child is young and not in your presence, set up a list of emergency numbers that can be given to any person whose company your child is in. That way, if you can't be reached, there are backup people who can be contacted. You could make up a card with these numbers and keep it in your child's backpack or give it directly to the person responsible for your child's supervision. When your child is older, it is also a good idea to have a list of these numbers somewhere handy at home, in case your child is unable to directly contact you when you are out. Include these numbers in your child's phone contacts if he or she has a phone. Get to know your neighbours and establish friendships with them. It is comforting to know that there are reliable people close by should you need them.

Filtering Advice

From the moment your child is born, you will get an influx of advice, wanted or not. This advice will come from well-intentioned family members and friends and even acquaintances. These people mean well, although sometimes they may come across as annoying and you'll feel they are interfering.

Everyone has an opinion and likes to share it with you, particularly when you are parenting on your own. It is human instinct to want to help each other out, and that desire also presents as verbal input. It is often assumed that you would welcome advice, and so it is freely given without you having to ask! This despite your politely declining offers. There you have it; alas the advice has already been given.

Once you are a parent, no one is immune to the opinion of others and how they think you could best parent your child. A lot of this advice is indeed very useful, as your child didn't come with a manual, and those who have parented before you have gained experience in the matter.

How do you know what advice to take on board and what to ignore? Your child has his or her own unique personality, temperament, and environmental influences. Thus, although your child will be similar to another child in the same age bracket, he or she will have many different aspects to his or her makeup.

I think you know your child best, even as early as when he or she is a tiny baby. Temperament is very evident from birth, and you are the one who will first recognize and adapt to your particular child's needs. Taking home a new baby for the first time in unnerving for anyone. There is a network of professional support available to you, from the time you leave hospital. You can get help on any matter regarding the general care and health of your infant. You can also obtain helpful advice from family and friends, although some of it may not be relevant to your child or your way of parenting.

As advice is offered with every good intention, it is best to accept it with gratitude and later decipher what works best for you. Trust in your instincts, in your higher being, as what feels right to you usually is.

There were some things I took a great deal of notice of before I'd even become a parent. Not yet a parent, I believed I could pick up snippets of bad parenting. I witnessed supermarket brats and tantrum throwers and thought that these children were extremely spoilt. Little did I know back then that I would have a child who behaved in the same manner. I remember being grateful to a stranger who came to my aid in the midst of my toddler throwing one of those tantrums in a shopping centre. She could see that the situation was distressing and was able to diffuse it in an instant with a soothing hand on my shoulder and some firm, kind words directed at my son. You could say that she was interfering and offering some unasked for assistance. I was very happy she did so that day.

As we know as parents who have an understanding of our children, there are reasons behind unruly behaviour—tiredness, hunger, inability to express needs or be understood, frustrations, disappointments, the list goes on. You know your own child and what the underlining issue may be. An onlooker doesn't have the insight you do and so, even when meaning to provide assistance, isn't always helpful. Providing the advisor has positive intentions and is not being critical, it is best to be polite, take what you think may assist you, and leave the rest.

At times, advice can confuse you or downright aggravate you! You think you are doing something the right way, and then someone who has a lot of previous experience (or even just a different opinion) says something, and you either begin to question yourself or feel the fume building. You may welcome the input, even adjust it a little to your own requirements, or you may carry on as you are, knowing that, even though you are an inexperienced parent, you will learn along the way. Your gut feeling will tell you what's right for you. There's no point in parenting in a way that feels uncomfortable for fear of not complying with someone else's idea or upsetting the advisor!

I inadvertently learnt some parenting skills by paying close attention to my colleagues' opinions and parenting styles. Emma left notes in her sons' lunch boxes each day. That seemed a positive thing to do, so l did the same, with a simple message such as, "Have a happy day. I love you." Or I'd draw a picture. When my son started secondary school, to save embarrassment, I left notes for him on the kitchen bench.

I gathered invaluable information regarding the selection of schools from other parents. Sharon, a mother of three adult sons, believed in choosing a school best tailored to allowing a child to express his or her individuality and not feel pressured to conform to any expectations. Even if l won a lottery and could afford the best private education, l knew then how difficult it would be for a child from a lower socio-economic or even middle-class background to feel comfortable among peers at an elite private school. As teenagers are quite impressionable and still seeking their place in the world, teens don't need the added pressure of feeling underprivileged in comparison to other students at their school.

* * * * * * * ● ● ● ● ● ● ● * * * * *

Following Intuition

My son and I were driving to the basketball game following the summer school break and ended up at the wrong venue. Already a little late and having been so excited about recommencing the game, my son became angry and distressed. To add insult to injury, when we finally made it to the right venue, he wasn't allowed on court as the game had just passed half-time. By this time, his anger and distress escalated, and we immediately left. Back in the confines of the car, all hell broke loose.

"I hate my life," he cried. "Why do these things always happen to me? I just want to die. Mum, stop the car and let me get in front of it." This continued—blah, blah …swear word …blah, blah, blah …more swear words.

Was there something more to this? We store certain hurts and disappointments. What else might be resurfacing here? After allowing his anger outburst and assessing that there wasn't anything more going on, and once things cooled down, I started that discussion: No Life is perfect. These things happen to everyone at some time. Although it's not evident at the time, there is a lesson to be learnt from such experiences.

I could feel my son's disappointment, and as a parent, all I wanted to do was put a Band-Aid on the hurt. Was there something I could do to lessen my son's pain? At the same time, I was in a quandary, not sure whether I should be telling him that he overreacted and his behaviour was way out of line or giving him some loving attention. I battled with what opinions others might have on the situation—what advice I would be given if someone else had been present to witness the whole event.

I went with my intuition. I decided to buy him a treat on the way home. It was a time he needed a little sugarcoating. Even though my son had expressed what seemed like an inordinate amount of anger, l felt that this incident might have highlighted other recent disappointments. So this particular Band-Aid helped cover those as well.

I felt that, taking a different approach might have caused his anger to be shelved and allowed to fester. I didn't want resentment or depression to take residence, especially in those teenage years when self-esteem is so fragile.

Some people may consider that my actions were unwise that I gave into unacceptable behaviour, a spoilt child, and that I should have reprimanded my son for his outburst. I may well have taken a different approach at the time. Yet something within pulled me back. I knew in my heart what l needed to do.

* * * * * * * * ● ● ● * * * * * * *

Conflict of Roles

I am my son's mother. However, I am sometimes required to also be his father, brother, sister and playmate. I do all the things with my son that another parent may share in, including those activities a father might be more suited for. I am his only playmate at home, and so l adapt to the role of a sibling or friend. Unless we are among other people or he has some friends over, then l have to be prepared to take on whatever role is required of me. Sound familiar?

Being everyone rolled into one person can be very frustrating and tiring. I find l have to pull myself back from snapping, "I'm not your brother or sister. Leave me alone."

The upside, l believe, is that you are developing a special bond with your child as you play these many roles. The downside, if there is one, may be that you let lapse your role of parent and let boundaries slide.

A child whose household consists of only him or her and his or her parent or guardian has little or no experience of how other family structures operate or interact. Without siblings, a child is not accustomed to rivalry, jealousies, or even parental favouritism. Depending on personality and temperament, some children require more attention than others at times, and some less. Your one child doesn't see this.

When other children are guests in your home, the dynamics change, which can be confusing for your only child. Firstly, we as parents like to be courteous to our young visitors and make them feel comfortable, especially if they have a tendency towards homesickness. We have to be careful to treat someone else's child with respect and not take on too much disciplinary action, if any at all. This may not sit well with our child, who may see the difference in treatment as discrimination.

In his primary school years, my son often felt he was on the back-burner when l took on the care of other children. He would ask things like, "Why do you take more notice of Tim than you do of me?" Perhaps l appeared over-attentive when l displayed good manners or the child in question required my attention because of his or her particular disposition. I would explain this to my son, as I never intended for him to feel undervalued. I could, however, see things from his perspective, and l wanted him to feel what l felt—that he would always take precedence in my heart over any other child. I decided to make a sustained effort to treat him as l would someone else's child. If I could pretend sometimes that he was a guest, l would be more patient and generous with my attention.

Our children are very special to us, and they should feel that way. Unconditional love can sometimes be an excuse for inconsistency with our love and attention. To overcome this, just pretend your child isn't yours, and you'll be on your best behaviour.

As parents, we set rules and regulations and form boundaries with our children. We need to teach values and respect so as to engender in them socially acceptable behaviour. Our job is to be their leader foremost, providing direction in which they are guided and protected. Roles can be jumbled in a one-parent, one-child household. The parent's role can so readily be transformed into the role of playmate or sibling. The child can easily become friend and confidant to the parent. It is important to not lose focus of your parent role. You are the captain of the ship; your child is only required to be your passenger. When you have something you want to offload or confide in someone, make use of a phone buddy. A child may not know how to handle the information given to him or her, or otherwise may be totally disinterested in such matters. Better to phone a friend!

What about the role of the missing parent, if there is one? We all have our own situations and, perhaps, arrangements with the other parent, providing he or she is involved. My child's father has been absent from my son's life for most of it. There have been the rare visit and the odd phone call over the past twelve years. I worried and wondered how this would affect my son. There were times he cried over the absence of a father in his life. I felt the best thing to do was to allow him his cry and be there for him to dry the tears afterwards. Without being detrimental to his father, I explained that some people are unable to take on the responsibilities of parenthood, even if they imagined that they could have. "Your father loves you in his own way; he just wasn't cut out for parenting," I would say.

By the age of ten, my son saw this for himself. Following a visit from his father, he commented, "Mum, I can see why you didn't stay with him. He's not a family man."

We would discuss other important people present in our lives and how these people have positive influences that enrich our existence, so that the absence of one person can be substituted with another.

We were lucky to have two such people fill the void of absent biological father. They were godfather and stepfather. Though neither of these men are currently part of our lives, they each played a dominant role in my son's life at the time. These men both loved my son and lavished him with undivided attention, and for this reason, they will forever be etched into his being. He recalls memories of them with great fondness, and I regard them as highly influential people in my young son's life and thank them for their indelible imprint.

Perhaps you too can think of people in your child's life who may mimic a parenting role—someone beside yourself for whom your child holds a lot of respect and affection. What you think your child may be missing in not living with or having another parent around may just be a figment of your imagination. Sure, children may wish to live in a two-parent household. But if their lives are filled with love, affection, and admiration, then it doesn't matter too much where or from whom that love and affection comes.

Your child may have frequent contact with his or her other parent; perhaps, you and your co-parent just live in separate houses. That can mean two different sets of rules, curfews, and parenting styles. Clothing and required items may be left at one house unintentionally. Your ex may be re-partnered, and step-siblings could be thrown into the works. All of this may be challenging as you grabble for some continuity when your life feels submerged in chaos. What you need to think about is the contentment of your child. What's important is that he or she is happy, well cared for, and receiving plenty of love from both his or her parents. His or her receiving that loving attention from any member of the family is an added bonus. Children will come to know what is expected of them in each of the different households and adapt accordingly.

Adjustments may need to be considered if, for any reason, these visitations cause any undue stress or unhappiness. A child has the right to feel respected, comfortable, and safe in his or her environment, and any deviation means that something needs to change. If co-parenting is available to your child, then it should be executed peacefully—free from any pressures or conflict.

There is no gain in condemning the other parent or making comparisons, as a child has nowhere to go with this. Not only do these kinds of attitudes create negativity, they also encourage disrespect and insecurity. Providing there are no detrimental issues present, you don't need to approve of all that goes on in the other household. There will quite possibly be disciplinary choices, house rules, and meal options you don't agree with. It will go back again to your rules when your child resides with you. You may feel that you get the short end of the stick if you are pulling in the slack after a returned visit. However, as long as your child is happy, all family members, no matter what wrapping they come in, who provide a positive influence in your child's life should be embraced.

Whenever possible, it is beneficial to maintain a relationship with your child's other side of the family if there is one. It would be a shame for your child to miss out on interactions with his or her grandparents, aunts, uncles, and cousins because you may be estranged from his or her other parent, don't get along with the in-laws, or favour your side of the family. Your child is also a part of their lives, and it would be unfortunate and unfair for them to miss out on sharing your child's life.

I felt it was important for my son to carry on relationships with family members on his father's side, and so we continued to spend time with his paternal grandmother and aunt and uncle. He is left with fond memories of his grandmother, who has now passed, and she was given the opportunity to continue a rightful relationship with her grandson.

Discipline

A child needs our guidance, and as a sole parent, we need to be persistent in providing it so that our children grow up to become socially acceptable and respectable human beings. It is the parent's role to set boundaries and a child's role to respect those boundaries. As parents, we are expected to lead our children—to define what behaviour is acceptable and what is not.

If you allow your child too much freedom, too many choices, or too few rules and curfews, then you aren't at the helm of the ship, and it can be left to sail in any direction. The only way a child can journey through childhood into adulthood and stay on a reasonable course is through direction, which involves discipline. Discipline starts with you.

Discipline is easier if it comes from two parents who share an avid interest in the child. Your child may be receiving discipline in two different homes, which may either be complimentary or contradictory. It could be that, even though your child has contact with his or her other parent, you are left to do all or the majority of the discipline. The ideal would be being able to share the responsibility equally between two parents who are in agreement with one another and who are respectful and supportive of each other's actions. When this is the situation, even if one parent has to manage a tricky situation on his or her own, he or she can expect the full support of the other parent when the incident is revisited later.

As a single mother of a son, I have received comments such as, "It's a shame he doesn't have a man to be firm with him." Another frequent comment goes something like, "He needs an authoritarian voice to keep him in his place." I feel that sometimes I need to be tougher or persevere longer than I would had I the support of another parent; there's no "wait until your father gets home" or stopping short in any way of full disciplinary action.

I think that, with the right backup, as a lone parent you can be well equipped to effectively discipline in all sorts of situations. For me, that includes reading a lot of books and articles on the subject and gathering information from professionals and other parents, particularly those well versed in the matter. It's also important to have a good support system—family and friends you can call on to help you out.

A child will only be receptive of discipline from people he or she trusts and respects. Children can't be expected to follow demands from anyone they haven't built such a relationship with. Discipline shouldn't come from a stranger or an acquaintance, as it will not be well received. Nor would it be appropriate. You may find that you doing it on your own looks to others like an open invitation to step in!

Discipline may differ somewhat depending on the gender of your child. Boys and girls sometimes need to be handled differently, and being of the same gender as your child gives you the advantage of having an innate understanding of how his or her mind and hormones operate. This isn't always the case if you are of the opposite gender! It could be wise to employ the help of a relative or friend to allow you some insight.

Doing it all on your own takes a lot of energy and commitment. There will be days where you can't be bothered, when you feel exhausted and long for someone else to take over. People who are co-parenting are able to put discipline on hold until discussions are had with the other parent. You too can press the pause button and come back to dealing with the situation when you have had a break and maybe a chat with someone who is able to help you through. In the interim, tell your child that there will be consequences for his or her behaviour—that you're just taking time out to decide upon the most appropriate consequences.

It is great to feel supported. I have been very fortunate and grateful to my mother, who has helped me immensely in the parenting of my child. She lives a good distance away. However, she has spent a great deal of quality time with us over the years and is always available by phone. Many a situation has been easier to handle because of her gentle guidance and influence. When I've thought my son could benefit from a male influence, I've nominated my brother, who, with three grown sons of his own, has had plenty of experience.

Hopefully, you too have people in your life who can be of assistance when the going gets tough or for the times when you feel completely burnt out. You don't always need someone to step in; sometimes, just words of advice or some reassurance will do the trick. Your support person doesn't have to be a family member; it may be a friend or neighbour. People don't always know when you are struggling. There are no prizes or medals for doing it alone. Reach out to others when you need to. They will be happy to help and even feel special to have been asked. Needless to say, if a person is directly involved in the discipline of your child then he or she needs to have built up a rapport and developed a trusting, respectful relationship with your family.

Talking about Sex

Sex is not an easy subject to discuss. However, a discussion of the subject needs to be undertaken as early as any questions are asked on the matter and prior to your child becoming a teenager. It is best to get in before young minds can misconstrue what they hear from their peers or through social media. Children don't have the maturity to separate fact from fiction or decipher what might be morally right or wrong, so any information that doesn't come from you or a professional could easily be misrepresented.

The sex talk should preferably take place when your child is a preteen, before embarrassment becomes an issue. Once the subject has been open for discussion, it is much easier to revisit it later on. You will need to reiterate certain things, and some topics will require more in depth discussion as your child matures through adolescence and beyond.

My discussion on the topic with my son began when he was at the tender age of eight and revealed to me that he'd kissed a girl and was worried, as he was too young to become a father! I tried to get as much said as l could so that he had some ground knowledge to lessen the awkwardness he may feel during any future conversations.

I have maintained an openness regarding sex and sexuality, in the hope that my son will be more likely to come to me with any queries or problems he may have than he would have had I not made my openness clear. He can't confide in a father, brother, or sister, so it is important that he feels comfortable enough with me to broach this subject.

What have I done? I have allowed him to watch programs that have involved sex scenes under my guidance from as early an age as he became inquisitive. I prefer to be present to explain and have open discussions, rather than allow his curiosity to guide him to seek out pornography at an early age. I bought him a packet of condoms so he could explore them. That he did, and once he was finished, the condoms became water bombs. I intend to bring them back into circulation later on. I have explained, along with the basics, that sex is better when we experience deep feelings for someone, that people's feelings and wishes and sexuality should be respected, the difference between right and wrong sex, and the importance of practicing safe sex. I have covered everything in depth and then gone over it again. My conversations with my child will continue as time goes on and new issues present themselves.

Titbits of information gathered through media and peers can be misconstrued, and adolescents lack comprehension ability required to make much sense of it all. A child requires a full understanding of all aspects of the subject when it comes to talking about sex, and the most informative and trustworthy information comes from you.

It is recommended that the same gender parent take on the role of sex education. What happens if you are a lone parent of a child who is the opposite gender to you? An established bond will help make the initiation easier. Perhaps you could set the stage by gradually beginning the dialogue at a time when you are enjoying each other's company in a relaxed frame of mind. Not everything needs to be said at once, and if there is excessive difficulty or awkwardness, perhaps the child's grandparent, aunt, or uncle or another trustworthy person can fill in some gaps.

You are the most influential person in your dear child's life, and you may be the only choice when it comes to sex education. Providing that education may require you to step out of your comfort zone and undertake some research if needs be. Despite any difficulties, you will be the most effective resource for your child, and by engaging in this delicate education, you will strengthen your parent-child bond.

The Drug Issue

We would all like to believe that our children will never be involved in drug taking. However, despite our best efforts to educate them on the matter, we don't have full control. What we can do as parents is help develop our children's confidence and self-esteem. Kids are more likely not to be swept into peer group pressures if they know how to say no and feel comfortable doing so.

Education should involve undertaking your own research on the subject so that you have the facts. Your child needs to feel confident that you know your stuff. You could start by talking about how amazing the brain is. Explain that the brain is responsible for all bodily functions and that our feelings are directly controlled by the hormones it secretes. All drugs are mind-altering substances, and in consuming them, we change our brain chemistry in some way. The brain is an intricate organ, and tampering with its chemistry can produce long-term effects, including mental illness and brain damage.

Alcohol and cigarettes should be incorporated into the drug talk. Your child needs to understand that, although these aren't illegal substances, they can cause serious illness and death. As with any drugs, alcohol and nicotine are highly addictive substances.

My son is forever telling me that he won't do drugs. Can I take his word for it? No. I can only prepare him by helping him build his self-esteem. That way, he'll be more likely to have the confidence and skills to say no. If he doesn't feel good about himself, education alone won't be enough to deter him from trying substances that may make him feel better. As a parent, you need to be in tune with your child's emotions and recognize when he or she is going through a difficult period so you can provide support.

In what ways have I prepared my son to hopefully steer clear of drugs? I have encouraged sports activity from a young age, in the hope he would find an interest in sport. Not only did I want him to have something to fill in his free time, I also wanted him to experience those natural highs that you get from post-aerobic activity endorphin release. His passion is basketball. A child's involvement in sports also opens up another circle of friends with whom he or she can associate.

I have invited kids over to our house so I can observe who my son is associating with and how he interacts with his friends. You can pick up a lot on how your child socializes—whether he or she is assertive or shy, reserved or confident—by hosting gatherings.

I have encouraged my son to watch anything on the television pertaining to drug and alcohol use under my guidance, as dramatizations on the topic opens up further discussion and can reveal the detrimental effect drugs has on lives. My son and I have talked about people in our own lives—family members and friends—being the victims of alcohol and drug addiction; we have witnessed how addiction can claim lives early or cause ongoing health issues.

No one is immune to drugs. Anyone could be the innocent victim of having his or her drink spiked. Inform your child to always hold onto his or her own drink when at a party or a bar.

Teenage years are full of peer group pressure, at a precarious time when your child's identity is emerging. If insecurities are present, a child may be tempted to take drugs as a means of an escape. A healthy self-esteem is paramount in establishing the skills that will enable your child to say no to drugs.

PART 3
Building Inner Strength

Co-Sleeping

There is a lot of controversy regarding co-sleeping with children. In some cultures, it is normal and expected that families sleep together. In others, co-sleeping is taboo. In Western societies, it is typically usual to encourage separate sleeping quarters for parents and their children from as early as infancy.

At birth, it is common practice to put a baby directly on the mother's bare chest (skin to skin) to promote bonding and to encourage successful breastfeeding. Nature has it that a baby is born with a walking and crawling reflex, present for the first few weeks of life. This gives newborns the ability to make their own way and self-attach to their mothers' breasts. If a baby is swaddled immediately following birth, this reflex is suppressed. Whilst in hospital, babies are encouraged to room in with their mothers so that this process of bonding can continue, as ultimately, if it all occurs as it should, babies thrive and are less likely to encounter problems under these circumstances. Even partners are welcomed so the whole family can bond together.

Gone are the days when babies were left parked in the nursery, only to be brought out by the midwives for feeding. Yet as soon as the family leaves hospital, the bonding process is often disrupted. The focus turns to conforming to what society expects—in other words, establishing habits such as separate sleeping arrangements (there's usually a nursery set up) and encouraging the baby to sleep through the night, which goes against what nature intended. Infants require frequent feeding and are more settled and content in the vicinity of a parent. Who in the animal kingdom sleeps away from their young?

At birth, a human baby is still very immature and has no reasoning or recognition of his or her whereabouts. Infants must rely completely on their senses. They are comforted by their parents' voices, touch, and scent. A baby's only way of communicating is through crying, and a parent will instinctively want to attend to his or her needs. At this early age, babies need to be close to their parents, especially at night when their sense of sight is lost. If left alone in a dark place without the soothing smell, sound, and touch of his or her parent, a baby may be overcome with a sense of helplessness.

Research has revealed that babies thrive when they are exposed to human contact. Kangaroo nursing—a technique in which the baby is taken from the intensive care cot and placed against the mothers' skin in a pouch-like fashion—was developed for the treatment of premature infants. It was noted that these babies' vital signs stabilized, their core temperatures improved, and they were quicker to gain weight than their counterparts who did not receive this treatment. My nephew, now a young adult, was born at twenty-four weeks gestation. He was kangaroo nursed, and video footage evidences that his whole demeanour altered during this period.

Babies and young children require constant parental attention, day and night, and if they sleep in a separate room they shouldn't be left to cry it out if they are unsettled. They need to feel safe and cared for, and if that means sleeping in the same bed or room as the parent, then I believe that they should. Cortisol, a stress-related hormone, can suppress immunity, growth, and brain development if released in high quantities. A child so often needs his or her parent for comfort and reassurance. Why should it be any different at night?

Co-sleeping is an individual choice, and it has been revealed that it doesn't cause any detrimental effects, such as insecurity or clinginess. In fact, studies have shown that children who sleep with their parents develop high self-esteem, are happy, and are less likely to develop anxiety issues.

It is important that all family members get adequate sleep. Sleep can certainly be disrupted if two, three, or more people are all cramped into one bed. Co-sleeping habits shouldn't lead to sleep deprivation or interfere with couple intimacy. Parents should do whatever works best for their families, and if they choose to bed or room share, they should not be made to feel guilty. Co-sleeping is easier in single-parent families, particularly those with just one child. There is usually plenty of room, and you don't have to worry about disturbing a partner. Providing you're not just sharing your bed to combat your own sense of loneliness, co-sleeping has some added benefits. It allows shared time together, particularly important for situations in which the single parent has a full-time job and is busy playing catch up when he or she gets home. If you have a child who's experiencing difficulty sleeping through the night or who is afraid of the dark or has night terrors, then bundling up with you will not only provide the security your child needs, it will also assure you of a better sleep. The demands of parenting alone are taxing, and so it's important to have a good night's sleep, however you can get it.

When my son was younger, he was afraid to sleep in his own room, as it was too far away from mine. He was scared that something might happen to me during the night. This fear was exacerbated by not having anyone else in the house. If we had a house guest, such as his grandmother, he felt more secure. I did a little research on who was crawling into his or her parents' beds among the children of friends of mine—those with both partnered and single parents—and found that it was still quite common practice among primary school-aged children.

I am all for co-sleeping. I truly believe this arrangement has health benefits. I remember as a child how it felt when my father crawled into bed with me. There were four of us to choose from, and I would hope it would be my turn. I slept on the bottom bunk, so my chances were good. I didn't care that I was shuffled a little too close to the wall. Nor was I the least bit bothered by the fact that his warm breath tickled my neck or that he snored so strongly he sucked in the curtains. None of this mattered to me. His arm around my body hugging me tightly conveyed love and security. There was nothing to be afraid of, as I was safe in my father's arms.

Managing Stress

Stress is a normal response to challenging, difficult, or dangerous situations. When we're in a state of stress, a chemical reaction takes place within our nervous system, which activates a response. Hormones are released; adrenaline, noradrenaline, and cortisol which heighten our awareness and alert us to act quickly. Everyday stress is healthy and allows us to work through challenges in life; it keeps us on our toes. However, accumulative or prolonged stress can have harmful effects on our body. The rise in stress hormones is only meant to be short term.

Our nervous system consists of the sympathetic and parasympathetic drives. The sympathetic (fight or flight) and parasympathetic (relax/ calm) responses should balance one another out. The fight or flight response is necessary for removing us from danger. Once that is achieved, we come back to a state of equilibrium and calmness; in this way, the constant balance of these two responses keeps our bodies in a state of homeostasis. If the sympathetic nervous system overplays the balancing act of the parasympathetic nervous system, then the body will remain in a state of arousal, which, in the long run, proves taxing on all bodily functions.

The release of stress hormones increases heart rate, blood pressure, and muscle tension. Blood thickens due to increased cholesterol and sugar levels, readying the body for instant fuel release. An increase in the production of red blood cells makes the blood viscous, which in turn causes the heart to work harder. If stress is short-lived, then the body copes well with these changes and will readily revert back to normal.

However, if stress levels are abnormally high or persistent, then the body will remain in a state of high alert, giving rise to eventual disease. Hypertension and heart disease are well-known conditions linked to stress; there are others that have a similar insidious link, as high levels of cortisol deplete immunity and endorphin production.

In a normal, balanced state, cortisol is essential to the body in regulating blood sugar levels and maintaining blood pressure. It has a direct role in immunity function and in the body's anti-inflammatory processes. If stress levels are high and cortisol is in overdrive, then the body's ability to normalize is affected, and it is left to cope with high circulating blood sugars and cholesterol, higher than normal blood pressure, and a suppressed immune system. Over time, this will have a damaging effect on our general health and well-being.

To keep healthy, we need to manage our stress levels. We live in a fast-paced world where the stress response is constantly activated, and it is increasingly difficult to bring ourselves back to a state of normality. Even following a stressful event, our minds and bodies take time to return to a state of equilibrium. We can, however, enhance this process with the right tools.

Life moves quickly, and as the old cliché goes, there aren't enough hours in the day to get everything done. Why is that? Is it because we feel pressured to achieve so much in so little time? Do we focus too much on the little things instead of what's really important to us? Or are we conditioned to feel that we should be getting on with things when we remain idle for too long or are overindulgent in our own pleasures?

We all know of people who are highly strung, who race around from the moment they get up until bedtime. And we know those on the other end of the scale, who seem oblivious to any form of timeframe and get through the day at their own pace. Who do you think may have the longer lifespan? The more relaxed person is not going to trigger the stress hormones too often. We need to find a happy medium, and that can be difficult at times when we're dealing with added demands on our time and energy. We all feel more stressed at varying times in our lives; it's how we manage this stress that's important.

Having a basic comprehension of how stress effects our body helps put it into perspective. We do need to take a certain amount of control to keep our lives in order. However, we should prioritize what is most important and what **is** least important in our day-to-day living. If there is one important thing to do or challenge in our day, then that should be our main focus. Anything else around it becoming less of a priority, even if that entails carrying something over to a future time or day. Sometimes we just can't physically get everything done when we would like to or when we're expected to, yet we push on because we don't want to let people down or to appear inadequate or incompetent.

Taking on less requires resilience. Ultimately, we serve ourselves an injustice by taking on more than we can handle. We need to sometimes say no and feel comfortable in doing so. That means saying no to yourself, to family, to friends, and even in your place of employment. Accept that it is okay to leave some things. If you have too much on your plate, you will quite likely find yourself overtaxed and struggling to get things done. You may feel that you can't relax until everything on your list is ticked off, and if that includes washing the car, you'll do it rather than postponing it to a day when you have more free time. It's not worth acquiring a headache in exchange for getting everything done. Your body is simply telling you that it's too much to handle. Wouldn't it be better to focus on what is right and good for you and not take on too much in the first place? You really don't want to take years off your life or run yourself into the ground, so slow down your pace. And thank yourself for doing so, as it will be you who will reap the benefits.

How can we minimize stress and create balance in our lives? We can simply reduce daily demands and change the way we think in order to lessen our stress levels considerably. We can't always achieve everything we want to in a specific timeframe, and so we should learn to be forgiving and give ourselves permission to leave it for another time. Things may be left undone, and that's okay. At least give yourself a pat on the back for the things you do get done. Tomorrow is another day, and maybe you will find time then or on the next day or on the one after that. If you have a task to complete that is deadline sensitive, then make that your main focus and shelve the less important stuff, accepting that to do so is perfectly fine and reminding yourself that your mind and body will thank you for it, as there won't be a saturation of stress hormones running through your system creating havoc. Your mind will be calmer, and as such, you will more likely be even-tempered and easier to be around than perhaps you would otherwise be if you were running around trying to fit everything in. Your body won't feel depleted of energy, and you will be more likely to remain normotensive and less likely to need a lie-down or dose of Panadol.

Slow down when you are sick. It's your body's way of telling you that you need to take a break. Taking painkillers, cold and flu tablets, and the like may mean you can push through. However, you are only treating the symptoms, not the actual cause. You can be tricked into believing that you are cured when actually you are not. If you dismiss your illness by not slowing down or taking time out to rest, then further physiological impairment may occur. This can affect your overall health by weakening the immune system, which in turn makes you more vulnerable to future ailments and disease.

Sometimes everything crops up at once, and you really do need to get on top of things with little time to do it in. Don't be afraid to ask for help. There's no need to appear as if you have everything under control when clearly you've taken on too much. You are the one at stake. There's no gain in falling in a heap. Ask for some help with the mundane chores, or just let them sit for awhile so you can get on with the more important stuff.

You may experience feelings of guilt if you slack off for too long. A lazy, slumber, stay-in-your-pyjamas-all-day plan, for doing not much other than reading, watching television, or spending the day with your child, may quickly dissipate if you think you are wasting time. It takes self-control to continue with your plan when your thoughts drift off to things you "should" be doing. You deserve a day to chill out, so if and when you get the opportunity to have one, take it. If someone ran you a hot bath and said, "You've been working hard lately; here, hop in the bath and just relax," you would probably gracefully thank the person and do as he or she said. There would be no point in refusing the offer, as you would know he or she was right—you deserve the treat. So be kind to yourself; if no one else is around to make such a suggestion, then let that person be you.

The sole responsibility for a child can add to your stress levels. Not only are you trying to cope with your own life's daily demands, you have to also factor in those of your child's. A nice sit-down with a cup of tea after a hard day's work isn't immediate on the agenda when you have a child to pick up and feed, homework to help with, and on and on. Time continues on, and it may be only when you climb into bed that you realize you didn't take time out for yourself. This then can give rise to frustration and dissatisfaction. You go to sleep vowing that you will make some time for yourself the following day, and hopefully you do. Unless you make a conscious effort to take nominated breaks during the course of your day, even small ones, your stress levels will escalate.

A day full of pressure and demands has a tendency to overflow into family life, and a minor irritation can be the cause of an unwarranted outburst. A period of self-indulgence, however small, can keep you on an even keel and prevent potential family upsets. It is far better to have peace of mind and a calm household than to linger on feelings of guilt because you didn't complete one or two or even more chores on your list. You won't die because the dishes aren't washed and the housework is mounting. Nor will your health deteriorate. However, it may if you push yourself to the limit.

Changing the way we think involves replacing negative thoughts with positive thoughts and, thus, adjusting body chemistry. Good thoughts instantly make us feel good. Conversely, bad thoughts have the opposite effect. Our minds are in constant chatter and our moods shift according to the kinds of thoughts we think. Every thought produces a chemical reaction. Sometimes we find ourselves caught up in automatic negative thoughts (ANTs), where negative thoughts spiral out of control, causing us to feel stressed and miserable and giving rise to a negative mindset and negative behaviour. If we don't stomp on these ANTs, they can cause our bodies to be in a constant state of tension, activating our stress hormones. Positive thoughts are much better for our well-being and should replace negative thinking as often as possible. In this state of mind, the release of serotonin produces feelings of happiness and peace, and our bodies remain in a state of harmony.

Training our brains to think more positively can have a tremendous impact on our feelings and behaviour and, hence, will lessen the amount of stress in our lives. There is also an added bonus; people prefer to be around those who consider their cup half full than they do those who see it as half empty. Optimism opens up an array of opportunities, improving quality of life. Simply put, positive thoughts lead to a positive mindset and positive outcomes. Pessimists feed on negative thoughts; opportunities are missed, and the world becomes a haze of gloom. People connect to those whose attitude is positive. Negativity alienates.

• • • • • • • • ● • • • • • • • • • •

Changing Thoughts

Have you ever woken up in the middle of the night and started to think over things? What usually happens? Worries (usually exaggerated) start to surface, and one thought leads to another. Before you know it, you have a case of ANTs, and it's difficult to switch off. By morning, you wonder why you wasted so much sleep time on your concerns, as things don't seem as bad now that you've managed to fall back to sleep.

Next time you notice this pattern, it's handy to remember that the process of sleep does work on problem-solving. Tell yourself that it is much better to let your dreams do the sorting.

Do you ever notice how your mood changes when you are alone in a car on a long road trip? Thoughts come and go, and the type of feelings they conjure up depends on whether you create a negative or positive slant to the thoughts. You may have been feeling upbeat and peaceful at the beginning of the journey, but by the end, you're worried and tense. As your thoughts chop and change, you become aware of your mood. Perhaps you also become aware of whether your body is tense or relaxed. What you are thinking will determine your internal chemistry. To make a quick change to a positive state of mind, put on some music or search for a comedy program. The release of endorphins will have an immediate calming, feel-good affect.

* * * * * * * * * ● * * * * * * * * * *

We all have worries from time to time; no one is immune. Life constantly challenges us. Some hurdles are bigger than others and more difficult to get over. However, it is only by forging ahead that we cope through adversity and learn resilience. Worry becomes a problem if we let it fester. We have to deal with our challenges; they are merely tests in life designed to enable us to grow and expand. Once we pass one test, another crops up. Yet we are able to cope better with each one as our inner strength grows. If we avoid tackling our difficulties, then we are left with feelings of weakness and anxiety. Chronic worry is a side effect of issues left unresolved.

Sometimes, worries stem from an overactive negative mindset; thoughts are tainted as the mind fabricates or exaggerates a potential concern. Not everything we think is logical or the truth. Our thoughts sometimes lie to us, depending on our perception of things. An incessant negative chatter clouds the mind of rational thought, and we can enter into a state of constant worry, spiralling downwards towards anxiety and depression. So it is best to accept and deal with life's twists and turns and not get caught up in the automatic negative thought process. Be mindful of asking for help with a problem or talking something over with someone, so you can deal with it and get on with more positive aspects of your life. As only your child is at home and you can't burden him or her with adult concerns, you may need to make a phone call or wait some time before that discussion is held. If that is the case, feel free to let whatever is bothering you go for the time being, knowing that it will be addressed when the time is right.

In a balanced state of being, the central nervous system is making constant adjustments, keeping us in alignment. When the sympathetic nervous system is activated, the parasympathetic nervous system comes into play, bringing us back into a state of calm. If we need to act or think quickly, we step out of our calm room as our sympathetic nervous system comes back into play, alerting our senses. Constant and minute adjustments are occurring all the time, keeping our bodies in a healthy state. Any upset in the equilibrium can cause unwanted hormones to remain in circulation. Stress, anxiety, depression and feelings of failure and hopelessness have the potential to keep cortisol at high circulating levels. Chronic cortisol stimulation will directly affect the immune system, which can, in turn, cause illness and a shorter lifespan. We all desire to remain healthy and achieve longevity. If we are our child's only parent, then living a long, healthy life becomes paramount to our entire existence.

Let's look at ways in which we can truly relax, switch off from the fast-paced world in which we live, deactivate alarm buttons, and move into a more tranquil state.

First, we need to let go of things we feel we should be doing and realign with our inner being. Give yourself permission to take time out, where there are no interruptions. This could take just a few moments of your time. Sit quietly, allowing your thoughts to drift in and out of your mind, soak in the stillness of the objects around you, or perhaps notice the wind rustling through the leaves of the trees as you gaze out the window. Just *be*, knowing that, for the next few moments or minutes, you can enjoy doing nothing. If guilt creeps in, remind yourself that you are giving your mind respite. Often, we fill our heads with endless thoughts and lists of things to do. If we allow ourselves to switch off for a while, we'll come back in a clearer headspace, suddenly finding solutions to our problems and with more energy and vitality to perform projects.

Meditation is an activity commonly practiced to silence the mind.

It involves clearing the mind of random thoughts and redirecting focus on sounds, visualization, and objects or simply breathing to increase awareness of the present moment. It has the added benefit of strengthening pathways and decreasing atrophy of the brain, thereby keeping it in top performance. Meditation can be undertaken on your own (but be patient; it can take some practice to still the mind). Or you can take a class or even purchase or download an audiotape. Yoga is another method used to induce relaxation. It involves a connection of mind, body, and spirit, unifying the body as one in harmony and giving us a true sense of balance and oneness. There are many different forms of yoga, incorporating varying poses and exercise. You could choose a class that suits you, seek a DVD, or download a video.

Other things you can undertake to reduce stress include exercise, engaging in laughter and humour, massage therapy, music therapy, hypnotherapy, and aromatherapy. There is also Emotional Freedom Technique (EFT) also known as Tapping Therapy. This therapeutic intervention works on unlocking emotional blocks from the body by tapping on the body's invisible energy pathways. As with hypnotherapy, EFT works on releasing negative beliefs and conditioning, replacing negative thought patterns with more positive ones.

You can, I'm sure, think of other healthy ways to relieve stress and tension—a nice relaxing bath, an enjoyable time spent with friends and loved ones, a well-deserved holiday, and anything else that works for you.

Never underestimate the power of the mind. The body will react to whatever the mind perceives as being real. For every thought, suggestion, or emotion there is a corresponding physiological and chemical change within the body. For example, we jump at sudden noises, whether or not the noise presents a potential threat. Notice how you feel if you are watching an action, horror, or thriller movie, as opposed to watching a comedy or documentary in nature. Do you feel uneasy and tense or calm and relaxed? Even though you know what's happening is only on the screen, your mind can't differentiate between what's real and what isn't, so your body will react accordingly.

I first became aware of the power of the mind as a child. As we didn't have any alarm clocks, my mother instructed her four young children to wake at a certain time by suggestion; we were told to knock on the wall six times (the number would depend on the time we were to be woken) before going to sleep. Never did this fail me, and I can still rely on this method. The placebo effect involves tricking the mind into believing that the body has been treated for a particular ailment by administering inert medication. A person takes a sugar pill, believing it to have pharmaceutical properties, and the body responds by showing an improvement in symptoms. The theory is that, if the person has the expectation of the medication working on the ailment, then it is possible that the body will release chemicals to do the exact same thing. Our beliefs and hopes have the ability to affect our biochemistry. We release certain chemicals according to the thoughts, suggestions, and feelings we are experiencing. If a doctor tells a patient suffering from a terminal illness that he or she has only six months to live, the prognosis will probably play out. If, on the other hand, the doctor suggests that every individual case is different and that quality of life may be enhanced by good nutrition, rest, and support (and or whatever else may be applicable to the case) instead of handing out a death sentence, then it's more likely that same person will live beyond the time expected.

If the mind dictates how the body should react, then holding onto negative thoughts will unleash all of those chemicals that cause internal mayhem, limiting our behaviour, our beliefs, and the way we view the world. Positive thoughts will contribute to a positive mindset, opening up a wide spectrum of opportunities that enhance our capabilities and lead to feelings of contentment and peace.

As the brain can't tell the difference between a real or imagined threat (the physical response is the same), we can train our thoughts and make adjustments to our environment. Bear in mind that what you view on television and/or social media may cause your body to secrete chemicals, changing the way you feel. If what you view is comical, then you'll secrete positive hormones; if you watch something frightening, sad, or tragic, your mood will dampen as negative hormones flood your system.

Social interactions can have a huge impact on your mental well-being. Hanging around negative people can be draining; spending time with them can leave you feeling empty and exhausted, as they siphon your energy. Encounters with positive people, on the other hand, leave you feeling uplifted and liberated. Try to avoid or at least limit your associations with pessimists whenever possible. That may mean downgrading your relationship from a friendship to an acquaintance or even eliminating it altogether. In the case of a working relationship, where it is impossible to avoid the negative person, don't get pulled into his or her negativity; remain detached, knowing that the person's negativity is coming from his or her own dissatisfaction with life, not yours.

Although you may be drawn into the desire to help negative people, know when something is unchangeable. How many times do we hold onto relationships, hoping and believing that they may improve if we just hang in there and be supportive, and yet over the course of time nothing changes? Let go of relationships that require a lot of work. They can drag you down. Why forgo your own time and energy, only to give it away on someone else who doesn't appreciate or even benefit from your efforts? You have yourself to look after, both physically and mentally. You are trying to cope in the best way possible with your own stress in life without having to take on other people's problems. Focus your energy on you and your family, as these two things are of utmost importance.

Stress will not only directly affect you; it will also have a profound effect on your child. A happy child requires a happy parent. It is difficult to be involved in the present when you feel stressed. Yet that is exactly where your child needs you to be. When life throws you curveballs and you're not coping, you are at risk of becoming detached from your child. Not only does this take away the enjoyment you should be experiencing, it also upsets the emotional bonding that should be occurring. Over time, your child will assume you don't have time for him or her, as your mind is constantly elsewhere or your energy levels are too low to sustain healthy, normal interactions. The connection between the two of you will break down, and your child will be left with feelings of isolation and abandonment and at risk of long-term behavioural issues. Fortunately, we have the resources to deal with stress so that we can repair relationship ruptures and step back into emotional connectedness.

Managing stress in our lives may require an overview of our lifestyle and making adjustments. Just as a car won't run efficiently if we don't service it, neither will we function well if we don't take care of our bodies. We can replace a car. We only get one body in a lifetime, so we need to be meticulous in its maintenance. Make it a priority in your life to take care of yourself both physically and mentally. Keep your body in tip-top shape by eating a well-balanced diet, engaging in frequent exercise, and acquiring adequate sleep. Take regular breaks—uninterrupted time out for yourself spent on relaxation or self-indulgence. Consider it a "body service." When we obtain an inner peace, our nervous system becomes more balanced. This will, in effect, change our perception of everything around us, enabling us to manage stress in more positive ways. In other words, stress can be minimized simply by remaining calm and thinking happy thoughts.

* * * * * * ● ● ● **◉** ● ● ● * * * *

Keeping in Control

When difficult times (particularly those that leave me not knowing what to do) present themselves and I find panic preventing me from seeing clearly, I take a step back so as to view my life as though I am simply an onlooker. In this dissociated state, I am able to regain composure and objectively work through my challenges.

If you can take the emotion—yours—out of the equation and imagine you are helping someone else through a situation, you can gain more clarity.

* * * * * * ● ● ● **◉** ● ● ● * * * *

The Pursuit of Happiness

How do we find happiness? What can we do to acquire joy in our lives, sustain contentment, and improve our general well-being? Is the true source of happiness a place deep within, or does it reside in the surrounds of our outer world? Or does the answer lie in a combination of both? What's certain is that happiness is available to us at any time, despite our circumstances, gender, or status; we just need to recognize it in its pure and simple form. If we are happy, our children are more likely to grow up in a stable, loving, and peaceful environment and, with our influence, be able to seek lasting happiness for themselves.

Happiness may feel unobtainable when we are under stress, which can undermine our self-worth and lead us to believe our lives are limited. We may fall victim to the misconception that we will be happy *when* … we have more money or more possessions, take a vacation, lose weight, get married, buy a new car or house, and on and on. You commonly hear the phrase, "I'll be happy when …" People postpone happiness to another time, as though it is presently unavailable. Conditioning, anxieties, and fears triumph over feelings of joy and contentment when we don't feel deserving of happiness. We are subject to the illusion that happiness is only ever transient, and when we do experience periods of joy and contentment, we are afraid to fully immerse ourselves, in anticipation of the bubble bursting. Happiness is not something we need to earn, wait, or pay a price for. It is here in the now; we just need the key to unlock it.

Health is an important factor in happiness. How can we maintain a happy disposition if we are suffering physically, mentally, emotionally, or spiritually? Our health is dependent on our physical and mental well-being. If we aren't right physically, then our mental state suffers and vice versa. So what can we do to achieve good health?

Let's start with nutrition. We know we have to eat to survive and that we should be consuming foods selected from the five recommended food groups. Keeping the body well nourished is imperative to health. If we eat poorly, all body systems are affected. Our body will reflect what's put into it; to maintain optimal function, the fuel needs to be right. Over- or under-eating or consuming too many foods high in fat, sugar, and salt and low in fibre, vitamins, and minerals can impair health and prevent us from living an active, enjoyable life.

High cholesterol causes plaque build-up in blood vessels, leading to heart and vascular disease. Fat deposits in cells lead to obesity. Too much sugar puts the pancreas into overdrive, leading to diabetes. Insufficient consumption of antioxidants (vitamins and minerals) can diminish the body's elimination of free radicals, causing cellular damage, a prerequisite to cancer. All of this leads to disease and, consequently, interferes with performance of daily activities and the way we feel.

How can poor nutrition impact on mental health? Memory problems, poor concentration, and mood disturbances can stem from inadequate nutrients or an over indulgence in unhealthy foods. A Western diet is loaded with an abundance of refined sugars and carbohydrates, which rapidly release energy into the body. More complex carbohydrates and protein are metabolized slowly, giving the body a steady release of energy. Sugars go straight to the brain, triggering the reward system; feel-good hormones—dopamine and serotonin—are released. As sugar is quickly metabolized, levels plummet rapidly, and we may experience mood swings, anxiety, and depression and feel fatigued and sluggish as our body comes down from the "high." This can lead us to crave the next "fix" so we experience a pickup and that warm, fuzzy, content feeling all over again. The metabolism of complex carbohydrates and protein involves a more gradual release of energy, and so our minds and bodies remain on even keel.

Feelings of loneliness, sadness, disappointment, or any other negative emotion may entice our cravings for those feel-good foods, and with the swift rise and fall in the accompanied mood we trigger, we can become victim to addiction. Soon enough, we may find ourselves stuck in a vicious circle of feeling bad, eating to feel better, feeling guilty for having chosen the wrong foods, and then feeling bad again, eating to feel better ...and so on it goes. Dissatisfaction and hopelessness creep in as we deal with our addictive pattern, headed towards unwanted weight gain and putting us at risk of obesity and illness.

* * * * * ●●● ● ●●● * * * * *

Choices

Replacing negative emotions with positive emotions can reprogram your diet choices. Instead of reaching for the chocolate or bottle of wine, your mind is in a happier place and won't crave those instant pick-me-ups. Stay tuned to what messages your mind and body are giving you. Your body chemistry is dependent on your emotional status; you have control over the hormones you release, which will affect the choices you make and your subsequent quality of life. Act upon what doesn't feel right or good for you.

* * * * * ●●● ● ●●● * * * * *

Taking care of your body also entails regular exercise and adequate rest. Exercise stimulates our circulation and immunity and strengthens heart and lung function. It helps shift toxins out of our bodies. During exercise, we release endorphins—our feel-good chemicals and natural painkillers. This, as well as burning off cortisol, helps us maintain a happy disposition and wards off anxiety and depression. Increased circulation enables better perfusion of all our organs, including our brain, which helps keep our mind sharp and, in affect, decreases the likelihood of our developing dementia and Alzheimer's disease. As we feel good, improve our health, and build up our resistance to disease, we demonstrate an increased vitality, giving rise to improved self-confidence, shattering limitations, and opening us to the fullness of life. Regular exercise will also improve quality of sleep.

Sleep is an important replenishment for our bodies. We need to rest following a period of wakefulness, to restore energy and to build and repair cells. The growth hormone is active during sleep, which is essential in building and repairing bone and muscle tissue. Children and adolescents do much of their growing and development overnight, so it is imperative that they get the recommended amount of sleep for their age group. The immune system is pretty busy at work during sleep, sending out antibodies to identify and neutralize foreign bodies and, thereby, protecting us from potentially harmful bacteria and viruses. As we sleep, the body mops up free radicals, protecting our cells from damage and subsequent disease, premature aging, and cancer.

During sleep, there is a non-rapid eye movement stage (NREM) in which our brain wave activity progressively slows down and body repair begins. Muscles in constant use during the day get a chance to relax, particularly the heart muscle, which, although never completely at rest, will slow its pace considerably during sleep. Dreaming occurs during the rapid eye movement stage (REM) of sleep. This is when we consolidate memories and emotion. Thoughts are sorted and filed according to their importance, and new information is processed, laying down new neural pathways necessary for comprehension. We can, hence, wake up after a restful night's sleep with a clear understanding or solution to a problem we thought too difficult to figure out the day before.

Good quality sleep requires conditions that allow the body to reach a level of comfortable slumber necessary for rejuvenation of all systems. Being happy and healthy correlates to creating such conditions, and having consistent, adequate sleep maintains that exact same state. In contrast, feelings of sadness, anxiety, and hopelessness can interrupt the natural sleep process, and a lack of sleep can exacerbate the conditions that caused insomnia in the first place!

Happy people sleep better and are rewarded by feeling refreshed and content. Miserable people struggle with sleep and fail to feel any different; in fact, their difficulties become exaggerated, as a lack of sleep compounds an already compromised mental state.

Insufficient sleep robs our bodies of "time out" essential for recuperation. Wakefulness is a time when the body is in alert mode, ready to make necessary adjustments according to environmental influences. Sleep is a time when stress is inactive, giving our bodies reprieve from being on guard. Cortisol levels naturally decrease when the body is at rest; paradoxically, high levels are counteractive to rest. There are times when the very thing we need the most– rest– is difficult to achieve as the increased amount of circulating cortisol keeps us alert. So it is important that the body is able to shut down, and successfully doing so means toning down the sympathetic nervous system, which keeps us in the "emergency room." Stress hormones also interfere with the production of serotonin and melatonin, both of which are necessary for relaxation and inducing sleep.

It is important to have enough of the deep sleep phases to function optimally. When we are lacking in sleep, our bodies will automatically skip the lighter stages in order to quickly replenish the deeper sleep vital for mental and physical well-being. When we are fatigued, our brains can't function properly, affecting both our cognitive abilities and emotional states. We have a decreased concentration span, reduced alertness, and loss of motivation. We become moody and forgetful and are at an increased risk of falling prey to microsleep (brief periods of phasing out or involuntary sleeping). Fatigue slows our reaction time, so we are at greater risk of road accidents, not to mention falling asleep at the wheel. Chronic sleep deprivation can lead to cardiovascular disease, depression, lowered immunity, and weight gain. Physically, our batteries run low, straining our bodies to perform tasks on limited energy reserves. We need sufficient sleep to recharge our batteries and to build and repair cells imperative for our ongoing health and vitality.

Happiness can be found in pleasurable activities and material gains.

However, this type of happiness is based on short term gratification. The more enduring form comes from a sense of inner fulfilment attained through gratitude, acceptance, a defined purpose, well-developed compassion and forgiveness (of ourselves and others), and altruism. Spiritual knowledge enables all of this, as we are enlightened to being much more than our physical body and outside surrounds.

Spirituality is a sense of connectedness to something bigger than ourselves—the universe, others, god, a higher power. It allows us to find purpose and meaning in life and be in touch with our intuition. It goes beyond our existence in this world to an inner deeper realm, which is ever present, timeless, and eternal. Spirituality is where love and peace reside.

Gratitude has the power to block out negative emotions and encourage positive thinking and behaviour, which leads to an optimistic outlook and greater satisfaction with life. Look for the things in your life to be grateful for. They can be as simple as the air you breathe or the eyes that afford you sight. We can all too easily get into the habit of taking what we have in life for granted.

What if something was taken away from you? How would you feel? How would you feel if something was abruptly taken away, something unexpected? Think of how you feel when you recover from an illness. You are more appreciative of the simple things in life. It's like being reborn and discovering things again for the first time, like you had perceived life through a blurred camera lens, and then suddenly everything comes into sharp focus. You have a renewed appreciation, as you had suffered discomfort and have returned to feeling comfortable and at ease again. Perhaps you have been awakened to the impermanence of life, and that all things, people, places, and circumstances are only ever temporary. You are eager to enjoy life as it is now, as you have experienced the feeling of something lost and delighted in its return to you.

Practice waking up each day being thankful for what you have and holding onto positivity. That way, you will be more likely to travel through the day feeling peaceful and content. Get out of the "right side of bed" and greet each day with enthusiasm and an exciting anticipation of what may lie ahead as the surprise of the day unfolds.

Be grateful for the role you have as a parent in the present moment, whether your child is an infant, a preschooler, of school age, a teenager or beyond. Soak up experiences as they occur. You can't go backwards, so enjoy and make the most of now. Let go of all the unnecessary things getting in your way. How important are they really to interrupt those precious moments spent with your child? Moments that can never be retrieved? Moments laced with laughter, happiness, and joy to be later filed as treasured memories?

Suffering is a part of life that we are all vulnerable to. Life is transient and ever changing. We will all experience loss of loved ones, illness, and aging. This is a universal part of human existence to which there is no immunity. We can learn to cope by drawing on our resilience, accepting that all in life is temporary and that we have little control over its course, comforted by the inner knowledge that love prevails; it remains deep within us, despite the unpredictability of our ever-changing outer world. People enter and depart from our lives, leaving behind valuable lessons, gifts of love, and memories to carry us forward. Illness can enhance our spirituality, and with age, we gather tremendous wisdom. We are able to rise above our pain of loss and permanent change with an appreciation of these personal gains.

Life is constantly unpredictable; things don't always go according to plan. Something crops up, and your whole day may change. Allowing for this helps you to be more flexible and squashes feelings of frustration and irritability. Becoming angry over intrusive events only wastes energy and stirs up negative emotions, opening up the gates of anxiety and stress. It is much better to remain calm, treating a new turn of events as an exciting challenge. Who knows? The change of plan may turn out to be a welcome alternative!

Stop and smell the roses. Still your mind and feel yourself in the present moment. Remember being a child and taking in everything, the now, using all your senses and simultaneously being aware of all that you could see, hear, touch, smell, and feel? Every discovery was magical, and the world was full of excitement. Back then, you didn't have responsibilities, problems, or regrets; you were just completely absorbed in the moment. Each experience was like applying a stroke of paint on a fresh canvas, creating a vibrant new picture. There was always something fun in each day. It didn't matter how simple the something was; nor did it matter how the day presented itself—rain, hail, or shine.

You were the centre of your universe, and your happiness existed entirely in the "now." Why not be like that again! Now presents itself to you. Live it and take joy in it. You once did this as a youngster; you can do it again. Subtract all the worries and concerns that surface. Tell them to be quiet for now, as you trust your inner wisdom to deal with them when the time is appropriate. Listen in the quiet mind; come back to the moment in hand. Entertaining thoughts belonging to the past or future takes us away from the present moment. Fears, fantasies, what ifs, guilt, anger, and sadness shroud us from the life we should be experiencing—the here and now.

We can remain in a dreamlike state, lost in our thoughts, creating our own sequel of life as we think it should be, and lost to the reality of the present moment. Although our body is immersed in the present, our mind is often busy dwelling in the past, trying to project into the future, or just caught up in a cascade of intrusive thoughts. This state of being prevents us from our true awareness, from using all of our senses to engage in our experiences as they occur. Our physical bodies reside in the world of now; our minds often wander in and out of the present. To truly connect to our senses, we need to align mind and body together. That way, we silence the internal chatter that subtracts from pure engagement with another person, being in awe of the wonders of nature or the elements of the earth, and being fully receptive to our intuition.

In fear of boredom, we search for things to do to fill in time—fold the washing, flick through a magazine, pick up the mobile phone to look through e-mails, check social media sites ...anything to fill in those spare minutes. Once again, this takes us away from the moment—the moment in which we could enjoy another's presence, experience a heightened sense of awareness by noticing the temperature of the air, or watch the dust particles dance in a beam of sunlight …just be. The simplicity of life is there before us, ready for the taking, and yet we can become so busy in our thoughts and behaviours that we become blind to it, disabled from deriving pleasure from the energy of the moment.

Accept your life and who you are without yearning to be someone else or to step into another's life wishing it to be your own. You are you, and your life is yours—unique from anyone else's; own it and be proud. You have your own special qualities, talents, and life path. Life has presented you with your own gifts and quests. Accept them; they are yours. Don't get hell-bent on what goes wrong or the notion that you may be living a life that differs from your desired reality. In fact, letting go of your desire for some kind of alternate reality, and embracing your set of circumstances can actually help clarify your life purpose.

Never undermine your abilities. Embrace opportunities—those infinite possibilities—as these will move you forward in life. Limitations will set you back. We are continually learning and gaining insight from our individual life experiences. The hand you have been dealt requires drawing on your special strengths. Refrain from thinking that life is unfair; it is for everyone at times. You don't want to get caught in the trap of self-pity. Instead, make the best of what you have and be at peace with that. Surrender to the ebb and flow of your life, and you will accomplish a more tranquil existence. When we experience a deep sense of peacefulness, well-being, and vitality, we exude an energy that attracts others to us.

Turn mistakes, regrets, and personal pain into valuable lessons, rather than resisting their presence and allowing them to conjure up negative emotions. They give us the opportunity to look deep within ourselves to change aspects of our being. This soul-searching can lead to a fuller, more satisfying life. If your reality is different from what was desired, so be it. Just as your fingerprint is indelibly yours, so too is your life path. Make it one of value, filled with love and peace. Negative emotions—anger, sadness, guilt, revenge, envy, and fear—need to be expressed and released so they don't fester inside and cause unease, which corrodes happiness, as it keeps us from existing fully in the present. Emotions are only what you feel. They come and go; they don't define you.

We enter this world bearing nothing. We depart taking nothing. All possessions acquired are temporary, and although they provide us satisfaction, they are not a true source of lasting happiness. Happiness is much deeper than that; it is being able to look within to discover your inner potential; it involves unleashing fear and worry so the moment becomes free and accessible. Enjoying life in its entirety involves loving and accepting yourself unconditionally, as it is only then that you can experience abundance, from which emerges deep fulfilment.

People who appear to have it all—good looks, wealth, and social status—aren't guaranteed happiness because true happiness needs to come from within a person, not from the outside world. We need to form a consciousness of our own uniqueness and how our perceptions colour our thinking. If we can peel back the layers of our conditioning, we can reveal an inner joy, untainted by self-judgment—just as we existed in childhood when the world was our playground, before we succumbed to our ego. Accepting ourselves empowers us to make necessary adjustments when life is trying and to not be deflected by a limited or distorted way of viewing things.

* * * * * * * * ● * * * * * * * * *

The Importance Of Money

Money doesn't make us happier when we spend it on material possessions. Eventually we will get bored. We may want more or to "update," especially when we are trying to improve our affluent status or keep up with or even surpass our co-workers, friends, relatives, or neighbours. What can make us happier is spending money on creating memories—holidays and family outings and a camera to capture these special events.

* * * * * * * * ● * * * * * * * * *

Spiritual growth is an important part of evolving in consciousness; the depth of our awareness and understanding. It is directly related to our sense of inner peace, and our ability to find long- lasting happiness. To evolve spiritually involves working through our failures, fears, insecurities, anger, anguish, grief, and other life challenges—through which we develop a deep knowingness and acceptance. As such, we can come to live a life of peace, letting go of our inner turmoil of thoughts pertaining to regrets in a life past or apprehension concerning our future existence. The love, wisdom, compassion, and empathy we develop as spiritual beings anchor us in the present to fully embody relationships with ourselves and others, where we are at one with our surroundings and connected with meaning and purpose.

Humans are designed to be social; we need interaction and intimacy with one another to promote a positive sense of well-being. To enhance our relationships with others, we first need to love ourselves. We need to acknowledge our own importance and accept every aspect of ourselves, warts and all. If we go through life trying to achieve perfection, we will be bitterly disappointed and become stuck in the mentality of "I'm not good enough." Through acceptance, we can work towards achieving personal goals of self-improvement and release any guilt regarding falling short of our desired goals or the desired person we preferred to be. Self-acceptance is essential for inner fulfilment, and in achieving this, we can go on to experiencing meaningful relationships.

True happiness is heightened by feeling connected to and enjoying the company of others. When we are involved in healthy relationships, we feel a sense of belonging, of being appreciated, accepted, and loved. We have people we can confide in and who can support us. These relationships make us feel happy, and in our appreciation we are kind and generous towards others, which in turn will elicit an inner satisfaction because of our good deeds.

Acts of kindness, whether they be directed towards a family member, friend, or stranger evoke in us a personal satisfaction. Examples of such acts include giving a surprise gift, helping someone carry his or her bags, assisting a blind man across the street, or giving someone a compliment. If we have a hand in brightening someone's day, then we feel good. And when we feel good, our bodies start secreting all those associated hormones, keeping us happy, content, calm, and healthy. The law of attraction applies here—when we perform good deeds, good things come back to us. Whatever we give out to the world will be returned to us.

Forgiveness is another major key to happiness. Holding onto grudges depletes from your love bank. It is difficult to maintain an open heart if resentment takes residence. You cannot change what happened in the past, how you felt, who hurt you, or what made you angry or sad. You have the right to acknowledge pain and regret. However, if you don't allow these feelings release, then you are in danger of becoming shackled to them. Allow yourself to let go of resentment by forgiving yourself your mistakes and the hurt that others have inflicted upon you. There's no need to condone another's behaviour (or your own for that matter). Just set yourself free from reacting to any associated anger by replacing your would-be reaction with forgiveness. Don't let grievances dismantle your spirit. Anger eats away at happiness, and the more it builds, the more decay it causes. Choose forgiveness, and you will find your way back to peace and joy, giving love a chance to flourish.

Unhappiness is a state we visit now and then. When we feel unhappy, our automatic negative thoughts become rampant, blinding us to any abilities and strengths required to pull us out of an abyss of hopelessness. We're in a ditch, and all that's in our immediate view is darkness. It can feel permanent at the time, as perception is lost, overshadowed by doubt, insecurity, and despair.

Life can be testy. We all meet with challenges that throw us off course, and when this happens, we are conditionally inclined to figure it out for ourselves before asking for help. Why? Because we are afraid to appear needy or not in control or to admit to our failings and discontentment. Thus, we battle for a while on our own. Perhaps our failure to reach out also has something to do with the very loss of our perception that's causing us to feel this way! Eventually when our suffering becomes too much, we may ask for help, reaching out to family, friends, prayer, or counselling. Doing so involves putting aside our pride and fear and gaining strength through the support of others and our spiritual guides. In order to rise above our grief, fears, and disappointments, we need to let go of our egos, which are blocking the way, and allow in help and a willingness to accept that healing will take place, after which happiness can be regained.

Be aware of how memories with an associated negative attachment, embedded deep in the files of your subconscious can be abruptly bought to the surface by environmental influences. These can catch you completely unawares, triggered by something someone says, something that catches your sight or a soundtrack playing in the background. Feelings come and go. Witness them; don't let them overwhelm you. You can allow your mind to dwell on a certain emotion, and it can change your whole demeanour. Or you can acknowledge it and then release it. By adopting an awareness of embedded feelings, you can allow them to freely surface without reacting to or passing judgment on them. Once on the surface, their energy can dissipate, allowing room for healing and creating a harmonious state of being.

Temptation can suddenly interrupt your thoughts, alluring you to behave in a way you don't feel is right or good for you. To help you resist temptation or break a bad habit, confront the suggestions that your thoughts present. Flick them away as you would an imaginary devil standing on your shoulder, whispering (sweet nothings!) in your ear. Hear what this devil has to say and then tell him or her to "Get lost!" Shout it out, reclaim your power, and turn to the other shoulder and listen to what your angel has to say.

* * * * * * * * ● ● * * * * * * * *

Suggestions To Enhance Mood

Music therapy, aromatherapy, massage, yoga, meditation, and exercise all increase endorphin release.

Adorn your home with pictures, photos, and flowers.

Take a bath.

Take a stroll through nature—a walk through the park or along the beach.

Spend quality time with family and friends.

Do something special for a family member or friend.

Do things a little differently. Change your routine. Take a new route. Make life more interesting by creating new neural pathways in your brain instead of treading over the same old track. (This can be useful when trying to resist temptation or break bad habits).

Help someone.

Give someone a compliment.

Give someone a gift (not necessarily of material value; it could be a favour or a chore).

Forgive something or someone.

* * * * * * ● ● ◉ ● ● * * * * * *

I wonder how often it is suggested that a person try yoga, meditation, exercise, natural therapies, and counselling to treat depression—before he or she is prescribed antidepressants. These medications work on changing the chemistry of the brain. Little is understood about how these medications specifically work. Their aim is to increase neurotransmitters, such as serotonin and dopamine, to help regulate mood. However, there is no method for measuring chemical levels in the living brain and no control over the collective function of the neurotransmitter targeted, so there are unwanted side effects.

Attempting to change the physiological chemistry of the brain by natural means is far more favourable than administering antidepressants, which potentially alters chemical signals that the body orchestrates with such intricacy and precision. Antidepressants should be carefully monitored in the severely depressed person. Mild to moderate forms of depression can be significantly alleviated through natural means or therapies, as mentioned above, and/or by a change in behaviour and way of thinking.

We need to work through unresolved emotions, and this doesn't happen through medication. Instead, these emotions just linger, buried in our subconscious and subtly affect our thoughts, perceptions, and behaviours. Illicit drug taking, smoking, drinking alcohol, gambling, excessive shopping, or overeating also suppress unwanted emotions yet fail at obliterating them entirely. These are behaviours that have the tendency to become addictive, and the emotions that they target just weave their way further down, where they settle and gnaw at the core of our being.

Drugs, alcohol, and nicotine work by altering neurotransmitter levels in the brain. Normal circuits are disrupted, as these substances attach themselves to the neuron receptors, mimicking a similar response of a neurotransmitter but disrupting normal pathways, leading to abnormal messages being transmitted through the network. Dopamine (regulating emotion and feelings of pleasure), which is normally released in controlled amounts, is overstimulated. A false relief or euphoria is experienced. Over time, the brain becomes accustomed to the change in the chemical balance these substances produce and reduces its normal production of dopamine. As the normal reward circuit is banished, the body becomes used to this fake reward system and requires more of the substance to equalize the same effect. A craving begins.

An instant yet temporary stress reliever is partaking in a glass of beer, wine, spirits, or whatever else you prefer. It is a certain way to instantaneously take away your concerns, worries, and depression by numbing your thoughts. However it will only ever be a quick fix. It is a way that many of us unwind after a stressful day and quite an enjoyable and relaxing activity if we keep our intake to the recommended amounts. Alcohol in moderate consumption can boost our serotonin levels. However, excessive and long-term consumption can cause or exacerbate depression by depleting levels of serotonin. Serotonin is an important chemical in maintaining mood balance, a contributing factor to well-being and happiness. Drinking to relieve depression, therefore, can ultimately lead to more depression, as the serotonin levels further deplete, leading to a vicious circle of drinking more to feel better. Alcohol is also a stimulant, triggering the sympathetic nervous system to release cortisol. So drinking to relieve stress may backfire, as it may, in fact, add to it.

Happiness is what we all want and rightly deserve. There are times in life when we experience great losses through death, divorce, separation, and illness, and we need time to grieve and heal. Happiness is placed on hold while we work through our anguish. It is often through these difficulties that we learn resilience and draw on our inner resources—through sorrow that we fully appreciate the joys in life. It is possible to lift ourselves out of the slumps during our healing process by being thankful for the love, comfort, and support of family and friends and by celebrating all the things in our life that are good.

Some people live their lives in an accumulation of pleasurable activities (short-lived) with no real purpose. They fail to seek out long-term gratification through achieving personal goals and, hence, miss out on the greater satisfaction that self-fulfillment entails. Sustained happiness involves setting goals. Achieving these goals gives us a sense of purpose and direction. To find your purpose, follow your inner voice, wisdom, and instinct—what you feel deep within the core of your being. Act on what you believe in and trust what your heart tells you. Don't deny or doubt what feels right.

You are your child's most influential model, and when you demonstrate positive behaviour, gratitude, compassion, kindness, and acceptance, it is likely that your child will learn to do the same. As a happy, healthy parent, you will be more content and less likely to erupt over life's mishaps, big and small. You will be present as life happens, rather than being absent, caught up in a trance of unrelated thoughts. Being fully present enhances connection with your child, and the better connected you are, the closer the bond you will have. Happiness is contagious. Your choice to be happy infuses joy into the lives of those around you. What better parent can you be than a happy one? That, I think, is getting pretty close to perfect!

Utilize the Power of the Mind

It's amazing how our mind-set can determine the sort of day we have. Not only can we accomplish much more when we are feeling energized, self-assured, and upbeat, but also things tend to go our way; they pan out in our favour. We feel capable and empowered. Conversely, when we feel lethargic, undervalued, or stressed, life can be a drag. We have very little energy to work with. Things don't go well, and we can fall into the trap of blaming the day for mishaps without realizing that it is really our destructive thoughts causing things to go pear-shaped. The very nature of limiting thoughts is disempowering. They act as a magnet, attracting dissatisfaction, discontentment, and disappointment in everything we do. The way we think will set our course of behaviour.

Imagine the mind as a circuit board with many lights and switches, and our thoughts determine which ones turn on and off. All we have to do is understand the labelling on the switches. In other words, we need to have an insight into our emotional status and the conditioning triggering our thought processes. Once we master our thoughts, we can take control of the switches, electing which circuits to activate.

The body will follow; the minds lead. The mind is the control centre of the body, and the body will follow its commands. Our thoughts will direct our actions; we can make choices. For example, if we want to accomplish x, y, or z by the end of the day, then we will be programmed to do so. This could mean that we hurry through the day, intent on what we need to achieve, with less time, if any, to devote to anything or anybody else. The control centre might demand that the body go for a run or take a yoga class; once the order is set, the body will obey. There is an attached physiological and chemical response to each of these scenarios as our thoughts set our body in motion. Consequent feelings of exhaustion and frustration or peace and relaxation can be attributed to the power of the mind.

Throughout life, we are subject to conditioning through our upbringing, schooling, and social encounters. We form a belief system entirely on what opinions we form to suggestions, conversations, and visualizations. Once implanted, these beliefs give rise to particular feelings, which determine our course of behaviour. Our beliefs can be so embedded that it becomes difficult to acknowledge that there is any other perspective, and we can become set in our opinions and ways of living. Old programming has wired set circuits in our neural pathways, and it becomes habitual to continue to use these circuits. We have, however, the ability to rewire these used pathways and weave new patterns. To do this, we need to change the course of our thinking, which can take perseverance and patience, as our minds need time to adapt to new circuits.

We can determine our reality by the way we process thoughts. Our thoughts lead us to the decisions we make, which in turn power our actions. It is possible to change our mindsets by rearranging our thought patterns. By choosing to let go of negative, destructive thoughts and focus on the positive productive thoughts our attitudes and behaviours change, manifesting a new energy and set of circumstances.

Notice how you feel when you are fearful, anxious, or tense. You probably note an increased pulse rate, tense muscles, clammy skin, and an inability to maintain focus. These are real signs and symptoms directed by your thoughts. Good thoughts can raise your serotonin levels and activate your parasympathetic nervous system, which keeps you calmer and happier. When you are relaxed, your noradrenaline, adrenaline, and cortisol levels are lowered, and your body activity is opposite to that experienced during the activation of the stress response. Once you change the way you think, you can replace tension with relaxation and bring your body back into a state of equilibrium and peace. The power is within you.

If life hasn't handed you the desired set of cards, then there is no advantage in playing the "woe is me" card; doing so will only limit your thoughts and, consequently, your actions. The best option would be to set new, exciting goals and challenges with the cards that you do have; this will attract opportunities and open doors that you would never have otherwise contemplated.

The power of dreams can be used to give us direction in life and to help solve problems. There is so much stored in our subconscious minds. During our wakeful hours, we predominately use our conscious minds to sort through our worries and concerns. This is analytical and critical and not always apt at giving us answers that are right for us. All of our memories and experiences are stored in the depths of the subconscious mind. The amount of information that can accumulate there is limitless. It is where our feelings and emotions (which form our belief patterns) stem from.

We can more readily access our subconscious mind when we're in a state of deep relaxation. This can occur during sleep or through hypnosis. Hypnosis is a state in which we are temporarily diverted from our purposeful mind, enabling us to explore the inner depths of our thoughts. We can acquire a more comprehensive understanding of life events when we enter the vastness of our subconscious.

Hypnotherapy is a process, utilizing the power of positive suggestion to bring about a change in a person's thoughts, feelings, and behaviours. It is preformed when the person being hypnotized is in a state of deep relaxation, the conscious mind is switched off, and the subconscious mind is accessible. The purpose of hypnotherapy is to undo any negative conditioning and replace it with that which is positive. The aim is; to treat stress- and anxiety-related conditions, break addictive behaviours, and boost confidence levels.

Sleep is our deepest form of relaxation, a time when our judgmental conscious mind is bypassed. Messages can come to you in the form of dreams as your higher, more intelligent subconscious mind speaks to you. Take notice of what presents to you. If you have a problem, don't waste needless time entertaining the conscious mind to take care of it for you. Think on it just before you go to sleep, and you may find that your dream clarifies the issue. It doesn't matter if you don't remember the dream; your subconscious mind will have been at play, sifting through all sorts of files, cleaning them up, and making you feel more at ease. You may even notice that you wake up with a surprise solution.

Getting to sleep can sometimes be difficult when your mind is racing. Turning it off means having the discipline to let go of thoughts or at least change their pattern. Remember that the actual process of sleep can be a remedy for rampant thoughts.

I would like to share with you something that I practice when I have difficulty sleeping (I hope you too will find it useful):

> There's no use in getting frustrated as you toss and turn, sleep evading you. Instead when you look at the time and think, *Great; only four more hours until I have to get up!* tell yourself that you will have a restful, revitalizing four hours sleep.
>
> Use self-hypnosis/meditation. Commence some gentle, slow breathing and muscle relaxation. Imagine your bed being extremely soft and comfortable and how good it feels lying there in between the crisp sheets, finally resting after the activities of the day. Feel yourself being enveloped in the comfort of your bed, and as you close your eyes, delete all worries from your mind. If this is difficult to do, tell yourself that you will shelve them until tomorrow, even nominate the time of day you will recollect them. Just let them float away, knowing that things may just sort themselves out during your sleep, or at least you will be better equipped to handle your concerns after sleep. When a thought enters your head, just gently nudge it away. With

a calm mind and relaxed body, you should find yourself drifting off into the land of slumber.

I am lucky to remember my dreams, and I hope you are too. Whenever I am under stress, I find respite in my "sleep life." In sleep, we create our own world, far removed from the pressures of our wake-time reality. Dreams have inspired people to write songs and stories. That we can fabricate magnificent narratives and picture intricate visions clearly in our sleeping minds when, if we were asked to create or imagine something similar in an awake state, we may have trouble doing so is incredible. In our waking lives, we most certainly couldn't conjure up anything as quickly and in as much detail as we do in our dreams.

That the brain can formulate perfect images during sleep when our eyes are shut and not receiving any visual input is amazing. It goes to prove that we can recall a great deal of what is stored in our minds. We are only aware of the tip of the iceberg.

There are many theories regarding dreams. According to a few, we are consolidating memories, sorting information, or receiving messages. Another has it that we are totally tapped into the vast subconscious when we are sleeping. Yet another says that, while we dream, the ego is at rest. Here the greatness of the mind is revealed, along with the potential of what lies beneath the surface. How intricate and astonishing is the creativity of the mind!

During sleep, external stimuli may shift through the senses. The mind has the ability to incorporate this outside stimuli by making it a part of the dream to ensure continued sleep. For example, someone knocking at your door may be incorporated into your dream story. The mind is very attuned, however, to waking you if there is a threat of danger or if you are in need, such as to attend to a baby's cry.

When I was growing up, I used to respond to my sister's sleep talk. I would wait until I witnessed her eyes darting beneath her lids before gently opening one of them to see if she was in REM sleep. Once assured she was, I would converse with her babble and play a role in whatever she was dreaming. The conversation became fluent the moment l interjected. I used to think that I was capable of controlling her dreams and was eager to ask her what she had dreamt of that next day.

The mind is powerful even in the event of sleep. Environmental sounds have an effect on directing our dreams. Playing some relaxing music will not only help you to drift off to sleep, it may also help create pleasant dreams. That same dream channel can be accessed by engaging in some relaxation before bed, such as taking a warm bath, massage, and meditation. Aromatherapy can also be used to initiate and maintain a good night's sleep.

The power of the mind gives you the ability to control how you feel, and with consistent practice directing your thoughts, you can form lifelong habits that will help you have a more satisfying and fulfilling life. Let go of anger, frustration, and envy, as they will restrict you. Savour happy thoughts and happy memories so that you activate all those feel-good hormones, keeping your mind and body healthy. Negative memories can surface unexpectedly. Allow yourself some time to feel them. There may be some unresolved issues that you need to work through; recognize these and then let them go. Give them snippets of your time for healing purposes and then direct your thoughts to positive memories and the good things you have in your life. Know that you can change embedded beliefs and conditioning. You don't have to live with them if they don't serve a purpose. Try some new programming.

Your child thinks that you are the best parent in the world. Yet you can think of others who seem to be doing a better job. You feel that you had better prove yourself before your child matures enough to pick out your flaws! As it is, you are his or her sole model. Now is the time to direct your thoughts, which will control your behaviour. Live up to your child's expectations. You can do it. You have the power and the determination, as your child is the most important thing to you. You can go about making the changes and adjustments in your world that will strengthen your family unit. Be the best parent in his or her world!

Lost Notes

Overhearing my ranting and raving (yes I do indulge in the occasional tantrum) my son appeared to see if I was okay. "What's the matter, Mum?"

"I've just lost pages of my work," I sobbed.

He proceeded to hug me, consoling me with, "Things happen for a reason, Mum. Perhaps it wasn't very good."

In my despair, I didn't see it that way. Panic overcame me as I scrounged my mind, pleading with it to just pour it all back out. Alas, it wouldn't. I could only retrieve small snippets as I searched through the depths of my files. For anything to come back, I needed to relax and think positively.

Okay, so the lesson was this: I should have backed my work up, damn it! No, that wasn't it. Perhaps it would come to me later.

I am not the first person to have lost notes; nor will I be the last. I read about an author who lost his whole manuscript when his computer crashed. My situation wasn't that bad! I needed to relax in order to open the channels of my thoughts.

Sometime later, when I calmed down, it did happen. Words came back in a flow, and although it took me hours to retrieve those lost pages, I felt I had achieved so much more. I was proud of my endurance and surprised that I could reconstruct my paragraphs with renewed determination. I experienced how the mind can be blocked in a negative state and flourish in a positive one.

There was the lesson! The power of the mind is all in the thinking.

Align your Energy

Once you become a parent, your focus changes. Your needs become second to those of your child. Your energy is devoted to you and your child, as the two of you comprise your immediate family, which is where your priorities lie. There are other important people in your life—family and friends to whom you are required to give of your energy. And then there are work colleagues and acquaintances, who also sit close under the radar. So who do you give to and where do you draw the line?

As you already know, you can often feel drained of energy when no one else is around to share the load. So you need to be diligent in what you are willing to give out. You need to keep enough for yourself to maintain a happy medium and to be able to carry out the responsibilities expected of you.

Choose carefully to whom or what you can afford to give of your energy, as you need to retain a substantial amount for yourself so that you'll have the ability to give to your family. It may feel awkward to say no to an invitation or request. However, it is essential to maintain some of your own fuel for your own well-being and, consequently, that of your child. It is your energy, so invest it wisely.

If you travel through life trying to do everything—to meet your immediate needs, those of your child, those of your extended family members, and those of anyone else who shakes his or her contribution can—then you may be doing too much and will eventually suffer burnout. This can leave you feeling resentful and overwhelmed as you exhaust all energy reserves. What you end up needing and wanting is time back to yourself. On reflection, you might kick yourself for being too lenient and swear you won't ever fall back into that same trap!

To redirect your energy and align it with your own wants and needs, you need to let go of any guilt you feel as a result of saying no. There are so many polite ways of saying no to people. Others don't necessarily know how busy you are or whether or not you are dealing with any personal issues that are burning up your fuel supply. So when they request something of you—such as taking on extra work, performing a personal favour, or engaging in a social encounter—determine how doing so may affect you and your family before you willingly give up your precious time. If it is something that doesn't sit well with you, then be honest by simply saying that you already have enough on your plate or that you don't have any spare time right now. Your reasoning for declining could just be that you need to take some time out for yourself.

Don't be afraid to speak up for fear of upsetting others or appearing weak, incompetent, or disinterested. Know that these feelings are merely your insecurities at play. You'll only resent doing something you felt pressured into or didn't have time for. Take back any power that you may have relinquished to others and use it for your own good and well-being.

It is essential that we look after ourselves mentally, physically, spiritually, and emotionally. All of these aspects require nurturing, and yet we can get so caught up in our daily affairs that it is easy to neglect our self-care. Exercise, partaking in yoga or meditation, self-pampering, or just indulging in a lazy Sunday afternoon is important when it comes to reducing stress, rebooting energy levels, and keeping our minds and bodies healthy and balanced. If we don't take the time to nourish ourselves, we will suffer, and our suffering can extend to those around us. We will have little energy left for our own needs, let alone to be able to give or share any with anyone else.

Sundays were meant for rest and recuperation. However, nowadays, Sunday is a day like any other. I'm old enough to remember that the only place open for business on a Sunday was the corner milk bar. Supermarkets, shopping centres, and pubs were all closed. This allowed people a guilt-free day of doing nothing much and gave the alcoholics a day of sobriety. Wouldn't it be great to have a nominated day of the peace and quiet that Sunday's used to once offer!

Sometimes we may find ourselves in social settings that drain us of our energy—interacting with people we don't really connect with, participating in activities that don't interest us. These circumstances may suppress us emotionally, mentally, and spiritually, as we are prevented from expressing our true selves. Instead, we are left feeling frustrated and disappointed.

We all know of people who have a negative outlook on life, and no matter what we do or say, there's no way around it. These people tend to dampen our spirit and sway our emotions. Be selective. Don't take on other people's problems, complaints, and negativity. Sure you can help people out every now and then. Just don't let them bleed you of your own positive energy, especially during times when you have enough of your own concerns.

There are relationships in which we consistently give more that we receive. When we have a choice, it is to our benefit that we decipher who we want to spend time with and avoid those encounters that drain us. We can't afford energy to be siphoned from us. Friendships come and go throughout our lifespan. Some people take up bigger parts of our lives than others, and it can feel difficult to let go of friendships we have formed familiarity with or attached aspirations to. Know that each of your relationships has come with a lesson that has encouraged your growth and that, once that lesson has been learned, it is okay for you to let go of those relationships that no longer serve you.

There are relationships that we can't discard; alternatively, we can make a conscious effort to block the effects these negative but unavoidable interactions have on us by choosing to keep our energy levels intact. This involves bringing our awareness back to our own energetic field and protecting it. We can do this by visualizing all negative vibes being destroyed by an imaginary high-voltage shield.

Just as people can negatively affect our energy levels, they can also make a positive contribution. We are naturally attracted to people who make us feel good. The reason we feel good is because they are giving of their energy, which we unconsciously absorb, restoring our own levels.

Just as we can extract positive energy from our surrounds, so too can we choose to share our own positive energy with the world. Leaving a positive energy impression strengthens our connection with others and builds our life scaffolding.

Energy requirements are substantial in a one-parent, one-child household. You may be fueled up one minute and depleted the next, following an unexpected tantrum or an unforeseen disciplinary action required of an unreasoning, defiant teen. Or the depletion may be the result of pure physical exhaustion, experienced simply because you are the sole caregiver. You make sacrifices for the benefit of your child, and you don't begrudge him or her for a minute, as you know it's all worth it. However, you can be left feeling empty. No one is reciprocating your needs. It's a matter of give, give, give ...take, take, take! Luckily, we have the treasure of unconditional love to see us through. In the interim, it is important that you seek out someone who can attend to your needs, giving you back a sense of autonomy and value.

Once your child has reached a degree of independence and maturity, you acquire a bit more freedom. Your child becomes capable of spending periods of time at home on his or her own, which allows you more time to do the things you want. This change of dependence can give you a false sense of security. Even though my teen loves being at home doing his own thing, he is still a child and mostly needs me around (for guidance ... love ...security ...and to police Internet usage, screen time, and the pantry cupboard!)

As a teenager, my son can act like he's very independent and self-sufficient, and I am sometimes fooled into thinking he can be happily left to his own devices a good majority of the time as he doesn't appear to care whether I'm home or not. I have proven this theory wrong. There is an obvious change in his behaviour when I have been absent for prolonged periods. It doesn't require verbalization. It is evident in his demeanour;

he becomes moody, distant, or attention seeking. I am aware that, even though he is able to contact me by phone, he is completely alone in the house, without the comfort or company of any other family member. As a single parent, you need to constantly assess where your alignment is and whether you are devoting a substantial amount of energy to being in the company of or at least close proximity to your child.

Life gets busy, and we need to make a conscious effort to slow down our pace so we can conserve enough energy for what is important in our lives. During my brother's recovery from a cerebral haemorrhage, I witnessed what transpired when he stepped out of life and then gently back into it. It was like he turned off the treadmill that was propelling him urgently through his existence. Once a man who was always preoccupied with his business and concerned about the little time in which to get everything done, my brother stepped out of the fast lane and into living completely in the moment. He made a remarkable recovery, and his priorities in life changed. As a mechanical engineer and racing driver, he was very familiar with alignment and balance, and for the first time, he moved away from the cars to perform his own personal energy adjustment. It was inspiring to see this shift and to realize that we don't have to constantly live in the rush hour.

You can set your own pace in life by setting some boundaries for yourself. That means being protective of your energy; having the determination to be self-serving; strengthening your worth, power, and confidence; and recognizing when your energy is hijacked, wasted, or misused. Consistently reviewing how we spend our energy by keeping track of how much time we devote to family commitments, work, projects, and leisure will create balance and streamline energy into areas that are beneficial to our well-being and happiness.

Thoughts are powerful. The conversations you have with yourself in your head will direct your feelings, and those feelings will determine where your energy is aligned. As your mind wanders, you can find yourself thinking of all sorts of things as you jump from one thought to another. You could be thinking about a person you bumped into at the supermarket, and before you know it you catch yourself analysing his or her life and problems—topics that are totally unrelated to you and your life. Having wasted energy thinking up possible scenarios that could improve this particular person's situation, you feel depleted, when in actual fact, whatever problem that person may or may not have (or solutions that may or may not be available) is totally out of your control and not even on your list of priorities. Keep track of the direction of your thoughts and the emotions you attach to them. If you find you have lost track of your thoughts as they divert in different directions, bring them back to what's important to you.

It is when we feel well rested, healthy, and nurtured that we can give to our children and enjoy doing so. We need to constantly keep well fueled by making a conscious effort to replenish our energy levels and to avoid situations and thoughts that unnecessarily diminish our supplies. It is far from being selfish to focus on self-care, as it is an essential component of our well-being. How can we give of ourselves if we don't take our fill first?

When we are operating with positive energy, we feel content and happy, and that equates to confidence and success. We vibrate vitality, which attracts others to our energetic field. Life becomes harmonious, as, on a cellular level, we are well aligned, all pistons firing. Challenging tasks become much easier when we have unbounded energy, and we have an emotional preparedness for whatever comes our way. What we give out to the universe the universe will return. Like energy attracts like energy, and if it's positive the law of attraction will be the gateway to fulfilling our desires.

Enhancing Confidence

Confidence comes from believing in your abilities and an acceptance of who you are. It involves a general sense of well-being and feelings of positivity. There is always room for improvement of our self-confidence. Some days we can feel on top of the world, and other days our confidence wanes. Concentrating on our talents, strengths, and successes can boost our confidence levels.

When you are confident, you exhibit a sense of control. You're unafraid of adhering to your beliefs and values, and despite what anyone else may think, you believe in yourself as being a valuable, worthwhile person.

Some people crush our confidence by attempting to haul us into a hole of negativity. They undermine and disrespect us, abusing our talents and capabilities. If we hang around these people too long, our confidence will certainly take a dive, as our reactions are generated by the emotions we feel. The more confident we feel, the more quickly we can see through these relationships and step away from them. On the other hand, there are relationships that inspire us, making us feel good about ourselves and bringing out the best in us. These are the people we want to spend time with; they compel us to them, as they enhance our self-worth.

When we are confident, we are more likely to take risks and set challenges for ourselves. We feel capable of dealing with what life serves up, and setbacks don't deter us; instead, we see them as opportunities that strengthen our character. When we feel good, admire our achievements, and believe in ourselves, not only can we accomplish more, we can exude an admirable demeanour.

A confident child begins with a confident parent. You only have to look around you to see that the apple doesn't fall far from the tree. Much of a child's behaviour is an emulation of that of his or her parent. If a parent has low self-esteem, how does a child gain a sense of self-worth? Your image becomes a mirror to your child. What image are you reflecting?

In a two-parent household a child has two grownups to lead the way. He or she will decipher the strengths and weaknesses of both parents, and perhaps these two unique combinations will balance one another out, giving the child options when it comes to modelling parental behaviour. With just one of you, the pressure to be the best that you can be is greater. Even if the other parent is in the picture, you maybe the parent your child spends the majority of time with. You want to provide your child with love, security, and confidence, and the best way of doing this is by possessing all of those attributes yourself.

To be giving of love, we ourselves need to feel loved, and this will be determined by the relationships we had during our own childhood. If anything was lacking back then, we need to visit our childhood to heal old wounds so that we can get back on the track of parenting with love. Seeking counselling may assist with this.

Our self-esteem may undergo knocks at times when we have an emotional upset; we may bear the brunt of a malicious comment, experience a distressing situation in the workplace, or have an argument or falling out with a family member or friend. It is important that we treat these emotional hurts as soon as possible; otherwise, they will stifle our confidence. It is only when our self-love is intact that we are capable of loving others, most importantly our children.

The gift of love is more worthy than anything else you can give your child. Beyond the normal parental duties, showing an interest in your child's activities, his or her sports events and friendships demonstrates that you are really interested in your child as a person and that he or she is worth your time. You cannot substitute by filling a void (that will be created if your child doesn't receive the gift of your time) with material possessions, no matter how big or popular they are with your child. Possessions may provide a temporary boost of happiness, yet this doesn't even measure close to the lasting happiness and fulfilment that you will be providing by being present and genuinely interested in your child's life. As much as some things may be boring or require an effort from you—frolicking in the sandpit, building cubby houses, playing monopoly for the hundredth or thousandth time, or shooting hoops with your teen—consider these moments as a valued investment in your child's development of self-confidence.

Demonstrate your interest even if you have to fake it. You may be present, supposedly giving of your time, yet your eyes are diverted elsewhere and your mind is thinking of other things. Your child is very astute at assessing your involvement. If we're not in the same headspace as our children, they will conclude they're not that important to us. When you allow yourself to be completely engaged, you may be surprised at how therapeutic this can be for you, allowing you to relax in the moment and to get to know your child more intimately. The atmosphere created will be one of shared love. Your child will feel the warmth of your presence whenever you are around, even when words aren't exchanged.

Teenagers like their space. This doesn't mean that they aren't appreciative or in need of your presence—despite what they might tell you! You just need to keep a respectable distance, allowing them their privacy.

If children aren't disciplined, they are left with no boundaries. They need an adult's guidance, as they are too immature to make important decisions or assess risky situations. Children feel that they are important and well cared for if they have some rules in place. Discipline is a lesson in self-restraint. If you give in to a child too readily, he or she won't learn boundaries and will be more inclined to go through life acting on impulse, not knowing when and where to draw the line. Not having learnt self-control, the child won't know how to delay gratification. When you spend quality time together, doing something enjoyable and engaging in good communication that involves active listening, it is easier to navigate discipline. Your child will have a well-developed respect for and affection towards you. Having an established rapport with children gives them a sense of attachment to family and helps them lay down their own values.

Encourage individuality. Let your child be the person he or she is and not what you aspire for him or her to be. We must allow our children to follow their own paths, accepting their choices and praising their accomplishments. As a single parent, or even a parent of an only child, it is understandable that you want your one and only to do well in life, and it can take some self-control to step back and permit your child to make his or her own decisions. We are there to help guide our children to fulfil *their* potential. They will love and thank you for supporting them without stepping on their toes, and doing so will boost their self-confidence and cement the parent-child bond.

I certainly want my son to do well. If I had my way, I would want him to complete a university degree. I have even chosen and suggested what I think he might be suited to (secretly, what I would prefer him to do). I have planted a seed in hope that it may grow as his desire. Realistically, his career choice is entirely his own. My job is to guide and support him. I figure that I still have a huge influence if I mother him well, building his confidence level so as to expand his vision.

Emotional security comes from loving relationships. Having our basic needs met and feeling cherished and important gives us a sense of self-worth. Strong connections and warm bonds that can be provided by family are the foundations in creating a healthy self-esteem. It is important to keep the love bank full, continually making deposits so that our children develop the emotional maturity that is critical in the making of a well-adjusted individual.

Unconditional love means accepting our children through their achievements and failures. When a child harbours disappointment, taking time to dress the child's wound with loving attention will enable him or her to move on with courage and dignity. When you show disapproval, you inadvertently alienate your child. To whom then does he or she turn, desperately seeking a source of comfort?

Make sure your child knows that he or she is precious to you. It is important that children feel valued by their parents for who they are and not what they achieve. Praise your child's efforts rather than saying he or she could do better next time. Listen to your child intently by maintaining eye contact and avoiding the temptation to interrupt. Don't reprimand, judge, offer solutions, or compare your experiences. Really listen by stopping what you are doing, leaning forward, and opening your eyes a little wider. After maintaining your silence and when your child has finished speaking, reflect on and summarize what he or she has said by validating points he or she has made. This will confirm that you have heard and understood.

When all this is done, give feedback and, where necessary, assist your child in making decisions or finding solutions, at the same time keeping the ball in his or her court. That way, your child will still have control over the situation with your guidance. Feeling like you have been heard and understood has the potential for diffusing big emotions and enhances your sense of self-worth and connections to others. Taking the time to listen and hear your child's point of view without judgment allows you to be receptive of his or her perspective, opening up the channels of communication and connectedness.

Our children are always observing our behaviour. They are constantly examining the way we handle things through our interactions with others and in times of stress and disappointment. They antennae in on our reactions yet don't have the maturity to analyse whether or not our actions are selectively the best. They just assume that they are because we are the parent and, as grown-ups know everything and get everything right. Wrong!

There are times, in retrospect, when we wish we hadn't unnecessarily embarrassed our child, that he or she didn't bear witness to our overreaction, rudeness, stupidity, or cowardice. We can't take those behaviours back. However, we can take time to discuss them with our child, explaining what would have been more appropriate behaviour. And, where possible, we can demonstrate apologies to the affected persons. Admitting to our mistakes demonstrates our humanness and imperfections. If we model this, then our children will grow up learning the same skills.

Practice optimism. You attitude and behaviour will influence your child. Make your attitude a positive one so that your child considers his or her glass as always half full and views his or her life as a journey of new adventures. In a positive frame of mind, energy is funnelled into creating the best out of situations, and self-esteem and confidence are at an all-time high. Pessimism nibbles away at confidence and narrows perspective. Opportunities are completely missed, as panoramic vision is lost. Pessimism can cast shadows on future expectations for your child, and he or she has many life experiences and challenges ahead. Optimism will broaden your child's horizons, opening a wide range of opportunities for him or her to experience and explore.

· · · · · · ●●●●●◉●●●●●● · · · ·

Mistakes

Sometimes when children make mistakes, they already suffer the consequences of their actions without a parent coming down hard on them. A child may be suffering from a hurt or embarrassment, and being berated by a parent compounds this, adding insult to injury. Make an assessment of whether the lesson has already been learnt and offer understanding and compassion. As a parent, we might overreact, punishing our children because we feel embarrassed or threatened by their actions, as ultimately, we fear that our children are a reflection on our parenting skills or lack thereof. In an attempt to quickly correct the situation, we take to reprimanding, leaving our children feeling unsupported and confused. There's no lesson in this and nothing to be gained. Instead, we deny our children the important skills learned through dealing with mistakes.

· · · · · · ●●●●●◉●●●●●● · · · ·

PART FOUR

Moving Forward

Dealing with Illness, Death and the Barbed Wire of Life

Around the age of nine to twelve years old, children have a heightened fear of losing their parents. My son was ten when I was diagnosed with multiple cerebral aneurysms. Having almost lost his uncle to the same disease, he was petrified I would be next.

I don't know why my child was faced with having to deal with the worry of losing his only parent. I can only think that having done so may have strengthened him for facing future adversities in his life.

The time leading up to, as well as the day of my surgery, was very stressful for my son. I had to reassure him that I would be okay (without knowing how I would fair during or after surgery but nevertheless keeping a positive attitude). It broke my heart that he was so anxious and that he had to carry this stress at such a tender age.

A year after my surgery, my mother, the next closest person to my son, was diagnosed with cancer and came to live with us for the duration of her treatment. Once again, my son was up close and personal with serious illness.

As much as it hurt, I had to let my child experience the emotions these situations brought up for him, reminding myself that they were a part of his life journey and instrumental in helping him develop compassion and resilience and an understanding that we don't always have control over life—it is what it is—and that it's normal and healthy to feel and express our emotions, all of them.

I myself had to surrender to these setbacks in life. I was powerless over these events, and I had to find the best approach to them. I decided to reduce my stress levels, which gave me more energy to cope with what lay before me. I realized that we can become stressed or upset over the littlest things in life sometimes, and when there are bigger things at stake, those little things fade into insignificance. We are all human; annoyances do get to us. However, when you are expending energy on other concerns, you don't need to waste it on crap. I understood the phrase, "Is that all you have to worry about?" And it became clear to me that, as a human race, we generally indulge in worrying about unimportant things, become easily irritated (how many of us suffer road rage?), and have a tendency to complain about something or someone, no matter how trivial the issue. When there is something serious to be concerned about, our focus changes, and we become sharply aware of what's really important in life.

How do we manage when our child becomes ill? Dealing with a child's illness can be extremely draining and take up every ounce of strength and courage. Your parenting skills can be stretched to the limit. If your child has a chronic or serious illness, it is important to be acceptant and honest; answer his or her questions and offer support, love, comfort, and empathy. All of this is extremely draining and requires every bit of energy you have. It is crucial that you turn some attention on yourself, getting plenty of rest, eating well, and taking some time out for exercise and leisure. This will give you some respite and enhance your coping mechanisms. Accept offers of help from family and friends, and if nothing much by way of offers comes forward, ask.

As the primary and possibly sole caregiver of your child, it is important that you get as much help as possible when your child is ill. Getting through daily activities is taxing enough without added challenges, and you require some nurturing yourself. You will need, as will your child, every bit of energy you can muster, so buy and borrow some from whomever you can. There's no need to feel uncomfortable or embarrassed about asking. There will be people who are more than willing to give you some help. However, they may not always assume you need it, particularly if you appear to be unflustered and coping. Remember that asking allows a person the joy of giving. Think of how it would be if the shoe were on the other foot. You would most probably be the first person in line to offer help.

The more educated you are about the illness your child is facing, the more empowered you will feel in dealing with it. Learn as much as you can, your child will feel in safer hands when you become an expert. Attend support groups if doing so is applicable to your particular case. It is vital that you seek all the emotional support you can so that you can remain strong.

It is always acceptable to express positive emotions. Yet when it comes to feelings of fear, helplessness, sadness, and despair, we attempt to suppress them, as society has failed to teach us how to demonstrate these emotions and to feel okay in doing so. Negative emotions are often left dangling, as we're not equipped to handle them. And when we do try to get a grasp on them, we often do so alone, hiding behind a facade so as not to burden anyone or feel weak, vulnerable, or inept. A person deserves to be able to express all emotions, good and bad, and feel safe and supported in doing so. When it comes to relating to people experiencing grief, loss, anger, shock, sadness, or confusion, it is best to allow them their feelings. Make yourself available to listen, acknowledge, and empathize. Just being present with them can be support enough.

Even though you instinctively want to protect your child from any negative emotions, you can't. Nor should you try. Of course, when children are very young, with little understanding, you can shield them to a certain extent. However, as they mature, there is not much you can do to hide or protect them when it comes to dealing with illness, death, and the barbed wire of life. Besides, they can feel very hurt and anxious if you try to cover something up. It undermines their importance. Children learn best to cope with their sadness when they are face up to it. By attempting to protect them, we prevent them from learning how to move through their feelings.

As adults, we know that losses and disappointments often open the gateway to new possibilities. A child is new to this, and you are his teacher. You can demonstrate how to pick yourself up, dust yourself off, and move forward to life's next event, being well prepared, as a valuable message was obtained through whatever it was you had to plough through. By enabling our children to experience the lesson of life's difficulties, we provide them the armour they need in future dealings with their own battles.

You can't promise a child that you're not going to die before old age takes you out. This can be of concern to both you and your child. From time to time I have had such thoughts. What if I have a car accident? What if I was to suddenly collapse? What would my son do if I didn't return home? Yikes, this can become scary! We have a choice when it comes to keeping fit and healthy and limiting risk-taking. All else is up to the gods. Apart from having some plans in place in case the unthinkable happens, there is no point in worrying about it. I think it is important to let your child know that you have his or her back and that, if something was to suddenly happen, he or she would have a number to call (or a neighbour to go to), and everything would be taken care of. We don't want our children to feel that they would be left to make any big decisions or that, if we were no longer around, they would have the weight of the world on their shoulders. Children need to know that, whatever happens, they can still be kids, without facing any big responsibilities and that their parents have arrangements in place.

You can tell your child that death is a normal fear, one that you also had as a child. Be positive. Let your child know that you are staying healthy and that you're intent on living a long life. Accentuate that there will always be important people in your child's life who will love and care for him or her, now and in the future. Focus on life as it is now and all the fabulous things to look forward to.

Life has its ups and downs. Yet we are conditioned to express our good feelings and suppress our bad. We have learnt to hide and be dishonest about our emotions through fear of judgment and guilt. How often are we greeted with, "Hello. How are you?" How conditioned are we to respond, "Good, thanks," despite how we are really feeling? The words just roll off our tongues, expressed before we even think. And just as automatically, we return the question. "How are you?" An almost predicted, instant response, "Good, thanks," comes back our way. Sometimes it is obvious in a person's body language and mood that he or she is absolutely not feeling that way.

Wouldn't it be better to be able to express how we really feel (or at least close to it) so as to release negative emotions instead of putting a lid on them? When I'm less than good, rather than contain any pain or frustration, I personally feel better if I can respond with, "I'm not too bad," or, "I'm okay, thanks," indicating that I'm not terrific; I have had better days. This allows me to lift the lid somewhat on the emotion I am feeling, giving it a chance of release. I'll take it further than this with people close to me: "Today's been totally crap," or, "I feel like shit." I know that the people I am most close to will completely understand and offer me some support. Total release! If we resist and suppress our negative emotions, we potentially activate our stress response. The more we can keep this contained, the better!

Have you ever assumed that someone you know has the perfect or at least almost perfect life? I know I have. This is really just a delusion. Unless you are living that person's life, how would you know? In fact, something may become noticeable to you, disclosing that the person you thought had a better life doesn't after all. The truth is, when you get a better glimpse at someone else's life, you come to discover that all people experience difficulties. It may just be that the difficulties of the person with the supposedly perfect life are packaged differently than yours are. When we are consumed with the unfairness of life—the "why me's," we allow ANTs to take precedence, which directs our attention to someone else's life (someone who seems to be cruising it), allowing ourselves permission to wallow further in our self-pity. We have the power to defuse those destructive thoughts by redirecting our attention to all that is good in our lives and by removing the blindfold so that we can acknowledge the truth—that we do not stand in isolation. Life, the good parts as well as the harsh and cruel, happen to one and all, and that's the way it is.

Isolation

As a single parent, it is common to feel isolated as you struggle with the demands of caring for your child 24/7. There is no one to share the challenges and no one to share the joy, no one else at home with whom to share stories or have an adult conversation, and no respite when the going gets tough.

The isolation is greatest when children are young and you are confined to being a constant presence. There's no popping out to the shops or over to a friend's house without child in tow. Invitations are declined because it's expensive to employ babysitting, and the cost of childcare is usually reserved for the days that you work. There can be an underling guilt felt if you leave your child at home to be cared for by someone else other than you on the days you have off or during the evenings. Frustration mounts, as, despite being single, you are tied to responsibilities associated with being a parent. Opportunities to catch up with friends are limited, let alone to meet someone new. All sound familiar to you?

Don't be disheartened. It's not all doom and gloom. Quite the contrary! There is limited time for yourself, especially when your child is very young. However, there are payoffs that compensate. During these early years, in the absence of "in-house" interference by any other family members, you have the advantage of building strong attachments with your child. You have a unique opportunity to role model according to your family ethics and values. There's no need to negotiate with the absentee parent when he or she isn't living in the same household.

Now an adolescent, my son continues to develop more independence, and I have more freedom. I reminisce over the early years, and my heart swells with love and pride—love because all the togetherness time has established an incredible bond between us and pride because I have been and continue to be the primary caregiver of an individual I have watched grow and blossom into a young man. I was there for that, all of it. I have been the one parent who has had the advantage of sharing every aspect of his life. Being a parent is the greatest pleasure, and I wouldn't trade it for anything. It is worth every bit of sacrifice. Sure, there have been times I've been tired, cranky, frustrated, and alone ... There still are. Isn't that how all parents feel, single or partnered? When you sign up for parenting, there are conditions. There are times when being a parent full stop is tough.

I remember wondering how I would cope as a single parent and, at the same time, being a little excited about having this challenge all to myself. It was like I had been presented with a parcel that I could secretly unwrap and enjoy the contents of. I could share it if and whenever I wanted. Being single, I was free to make decisions on my own without consultation, and I didn't have to divide my attention with a spouse. I was fully in charge of finances, school choices, family outings, bedtimes, and disciplinary action (I am sure my son is happy there is only one parent to contend with on this last one).

Help came out of the woodwork when I least expected it. I was surprised at how generous people were in offering their assistance, and it reaffirmed to me the kindness of humanity. The challenges I faced were rewarded with satisfaction derived from my achievements. I found a way to do things I would have copped out of if I'd had a spouse. This made me feel good and revealed my new or rather hidden talents. I have proven that I am capable of making wise decisions and have enjoyed the freedom of exploring who I am.

Your child observes your self-sufficiency in decision-making and in being able to manage a job, household finances, and all the required parenting roles you take on solo. This encourages him or her to grow up confidently, making decisions of his or her own and learning how to multitask. Your continued demonstration of confidence in your capabilities will also intensify the respect your child has for you.

Without taking away their rights of childhood, children may take on extra roles in single-parent families, which boost their maturity. They may be required to help with decision-making and certain chores that otherwise would be allocated to another adult of the household. My son has been an active participant in the decisions pertaining to holidays and weekends away. Had I remained with his father, we would have consulted together, made a decision, and then informed our son of our family plans. As my son has a greater knowledge of cars than I do, I allowed him to choose which new family car we'd buy when he was twelve. He did the research and consulted with me, and then I took over the adult role in the purchase.

To help overcome the isolation I felt in the early years, I attempted to expand my interactive environment. Being with a little one all day can be pretty mundane. Loneliness can creep in, especially during the quiet evening time when your child is asleep and there's no other company at home. It was important that I had some adult stimulation and that my child had some playmates. Joining some playgroups, organizing days out with friends with young children, and belonging to a single parents group was perfect for this. When I didn't have the option of anyone else's company, I would go to playgrounds and play centres and hang out at McDonald's. There, my son and I would find companions. And if we didn't, at least it would be a change of environment, where we could both be happy doing our own thing, isolated yet together.

As I have mentioned, a single parents group was a tremendous outlet. There was the option of weekends away with other families and evening outings. I organized a weekly pub meal on a Wednesday night with the single-parent families in my area. It was great. The kids would flock to the play area, leaving us adults to enjoy some mostly uninterrupted conversation.

Don't be swayed by a lack of motivation—by being too tired or too poor to get out and about. Your interests may have changed, and you may fear that your social skills have plummeted since you are predominately spending most of your time with a child. Being among others is very uplifting for your morale, regardless of whether or not you are the "social extrovert." When you are housebound take up a project to keep you stimulated. Maybe plant a vegetable garden with your child and watch it grow.

There is a fallacy that only children miss out when they don't have siblings. Cousins, neighbours, and friends can fill this void. An only child has the advantage of quiet solitude and peace and doesn't have to deal with sibling rivalry, jealousy, or competition. Before school age, it is important that children do interact with other little people so that they begin to develop social skills.

Being your only offspring, your child may worry about taking on the sole responsibility of your care when you become ill or elderly. Inform your child that you will have some strategies in place so that this won't become a burden for him or her. Make early plans so that you have some people lined up already. When it comes time for you to depart this world, your child may have his or her own family, extended family, or at least close friends to support him or her. Once again, coming from a home filled with love and warmth will encourage self-esteem, which in turn will make forming close relationships easier.

Embrace the simple things in life and be grateful for what you have in hand—a child you have the honour of raising and loving. The hardships along the way are due to your ego taking precedence. The sacrifices you make as a parent ruffle the feathers of your ego. Before your child came into being, your ego had the liberty of being forefront, and it sometimes struggles to operate from the backbench. Make sure you give way to it from time to time. You need to spoil and nurture yourself; doing so is a vital part of maintaining parental competency and, of course, your own sanity! Isolation, loneliness, and exhaustion don't have to be factors associated with single parenting. These can be overcome by taking good care of yourself and building up your community network.

Letting Go

Empty nest ... I peer at the photos on the refrigerator. The years move by quickly. People always tell you that, and then it becomes true. I wonder when my child will move out ... I would like to suspend just another ten to twenty years!

In a few short years, it will happen. My child will move on. I will have completed my duty of raising him. I hope that I will continue to be very much involved in his life, at the same time allowing him his autonomy, and I hope that my guidance and love strengthens and protects him. Like you, I want my child to pursue his own goals and dreams, to live his life with lashings of self-confidence, to be healthy and happy, and to find and behold meaningful relationships. In a nutshell, I want the best for him.

When your child moves through the stages of life, you have to savour every moment, as he or she is your one and only. When my son was a toddler, I missed the baby. When he was a primary schoolkid, I missed the toddler. When he was a teen, I missed the child. And I'm sure that, when he is an adult, I'll miss it all! I wish I could have each of those stages back.

If we had other children, we would feel the pinch of the empty nest each time one of them left home, so that, by the time, the last one left, it wouldn't come as such a shock. Think about all the little chapters throughout our children's lives that come to a conclusion. We have already experienced a sense of loss and grief each time our child passes through evolving stages—the completion of visits to the maternal and child health nurse; the end of playgroups; the completion of kindergarten; the graduations from primary school, secondary school, and university. And then there's all the stuff in between—the completion of music classes, karate classes, dance lessons, gymnastics, tennis lessons, sports training and games, and on and on. There are times when you feel sad, as whatever your child is completing concludes a part of your life as well. You become accustomed to the familiarity, the running around, and the people you see and meet along the way and all the little idiosyncrasies attached. When one door closes, another opens, and it starts all over again. You may feel a twinge of pain following change and then excitement again as new ventures begin.

When it comes time for my son to move on and create his own independent life, I hope that the way I have parented him has fulfilled all of his needs of love and security so that he can branch out into adult life with confidence and maturity. I am already planning for the big event. It is inevitable. So it is best that I have some tools in place to deal with the isolation I will feel and, most important, that my son will be well equipped for a life outside the confines of this one.

I want my son to move out when he feels ready, not because he is unhappy at home or worried about leaving me. As much as his leaving will be a sad time for me, I will also be happy that my son has reached that level of independence and excited for him as he begins his journey into adulthood. I want him to feel that I will be okay without him—that I have a fulfilling life, independent of whether we share the same roof or not.

What we all want is to help make our children's transition from childhood into adulthood an easy one and, without being suffocating, to remain very much a part of our child's life. Successfully doing this depends greatly on how we've parented our children starting from the very beginning.

Encouraging independence and responsibility in our children as early as possible will help them thrive. We have to be diligent in doing this, as an only child never moves up the ranks of the pecking order. With other children present in the family, the eldest naturally takes on more responsibility, as the young members require more assistance and parental attention. It becomes habit to just keep on doing things for your only child, and whilst you are "spoon feeding" your teen, you are still maintaining the role of "parent assisting child" that you may one day be afraid of losing.

As our children gain independence, we need to step back without hovering over or checking on them too frequently. This takes patience and perseverance. Still very much reliant on our love, guidance, protection, and support, our children will move through the stages of becoming more and more independent. It is our duty of care to loosen the reins and allow them the autonomy they need. Even when it is evident that your child will make mistakes, you have to allow it. Stepping in for the rescue isn't a way of protecting a child; it is a way of deterring his or her learning process. It can be very frustrating for a child to have a parent interfere with his or her emerging independence. The parent may feel the need to provide padding to soften the child's fall; the child just sees it as stumbling blocks placed in his or her way.

The best opportunities for growth are those that occur when a child is free to explore the world for him or herself. We know through our own experiences of making mistakes that they are instrumental in our development of resilience. Children need to process the discomfort of life going wrong to be able to develop the skills of buffering the intermittent blows to their self-esteem. As a parent, you will always have your child's back and be there for support and guidance. However, your child needs to find his or her own feet, and that will entail a few stumbles and falls along the way. It's easier to build strong children than it is to repair broken adults.

As we are programmed to react to emotional words, we sometimes find that we react before thinking, especially when we are out of alignment. There's little perspective left when we are tired, frustrated, or swept up in our own emotions, and so when we become involved in an argument with our child, we lose all sense of reasoning. We overreact, fighting back. Lost in the madness of our thinking (or rather not thinking rationally), we succumb to behaving like a child, losing all power as a parent. A child has nowhere to go with this; his or her only "recourse" is to feel disconnected and distressed.

Regaining our child's trust requires communication. Understanding the reasons for our outburst helps our child make sense of it. If we are to act like the mature adult, we need to admit to our wrongdoings. Children learn just as well from our errors as they do from the things we do right. Confessing to our misdemeanours teaches them an important lesson and clears the air necessary for retrieving closeness. If we don't correct and take responsibility for our faults, then our child may one day make a sudden departure following a relationship rupture, leaving home prematurely.

Building trust and good communication is imperative in developing a continued, long-term, resonate connection with our children well after they have left home and embarked on their own lives. Even when we are physically separated, we can then still feel that same strong connection as we would in each other's presence. When we are attuned to one another, we are always present in each other's minds. This in itself keeps the empty nest warm.

The years go by, and we can be very busy, always doing for our children—so much so that we simply forget to just enjoy them. Being a dependable parent means spending focused time with your child and not breaking promises. Build trust and carry out what you say you'll do. Be there on time. Surprise your child with an unexpected something—perhaps a ride home when he or she was expected to catch the bus; throw in a pizza along the way. You want to build rapport that lasts a lifetime.

As single parents, we have to be careful to allow our children the freedom to be the child and not expect anything beyond our child's maturity or capabilities. In the absence of another person in the house, sometimes we may smother our children or lean on them in an attempt to fulfil our own needs. Although our doing so is mostly unintentional, we need to be very diligent; we must recognize this behaviour and immediately withdraw, so as not to hinder our children's emotional or psychological development.

Whilst your child loves your attention, too much of it can be overbearing. It places too much pressure on the child to have to continually please and inhibits his or her autonomy. Childhood is a life stage of growing and maturing, fostered by a guardian (usually a parent). A child has not acquired the necessary life experiences to be expected to simulate adult roles or responsibilities. Children are supposed to be free of the demands and concerns of the adult world and left to learn to deal with their own issues—peer group pressure, school politics, appearance, and so on. Children need to grow and mature, steadily sorting through their own stuff. If we rely on children to take on other tasks, usually of an adult nature, or lean on them for emotional support, we rob them of their carefree lifestyle and burden them with matters that are inappropriate for their level of maturity. When a child is thusly burdened, eventually, his or her cart will tip over. The child may become resentful of having less time to do kids things and feel defeated, as he or she hasn't the capabilities required for the jobs assigned to him or her.

When do we take our hands off the steering wheel and release our children into independent life? When is it okay for my son to make decisions entirely by himself? Is it at the age of eighteen (too tender I think, even though, at that age, children have adult rights)? Twenty-one (when young adults have more adult rights but remain immature)? How about twenty-five? (This is the average age of maturity of the brain, so I consider children adults at this point, bearing in mind that decision making can still be immature as at this age their adult experiences are limited). I don't really have the answer. All I know is that the brain keeps making new connections and neurons; that experience instigates this process; and that, before maturity of the brain, the prefrontal cortex, necessary for logic and reasoning, is still undergoing development. All the more reason for maintaining strong connections so that, after being crowned a legal adult (which, in my opinion happens when children are far too young), your child will still come to you for guidance, drawing on your wisdom to help him or her make decisions.

When you have done the best you can in raising your child, you will have more confidence when it is time for him or her to leave. Sometimes you go out on a limb when it comes to decision-making, even with the consultation of others. Trust in your gut feelings and unleash your child, allowing an emergence of independence at age appropriate times. Love your children unconditionally, creating memories of warmth and affection they can take with them. Then, when they think back on childhood, although they won't remember every detail, they will remember the atmosphere of home as being a place of harmony and love. My wish is to get it right so that my son will readily come back and be involved in my life when he is grown and fully independent and, in the interim when he is finding his feet, have a safe haven to which he can return.

Purpose

A sense of purpose adds meaning to our life. Purpose involves our personal values and desires and gives us the sense that there is meaning to our existence, that we can make a difference in the world. When we connect to a purpose to guide our actions, we experience a deep fulfilment, one that enhances our level of happiness. Without purpose, we drift through life directionless, waiting for things to happen rather than taking life by the reins and creating our own events.

As a single parent, your sole purpose may be focused on your child—creating a stable, loving environment; providing good education; and instilling family values so that your child can find his or her own direction in life, being equipped with confidence and self-worth. Other goals may be temporarily shelved, purely because you can't give other projects the time and energy required. Your purpose is not necessarily limited to one goal; you could be working towards achieving several goals, all on the go at the same time, depending on your life circumstances.

As challenging as it is, pleasurable some days and some days not, rewarding and frustrating, parenthood does add meaning and purpose to your life. There will be times when your child is away from home—at camp, visiting the other parent, at sleepovers with friends or relatives, and on social outings. He or she will eventually gain more independence and move out of home for good. The role you have mastered for so many years will undergo a major shift, and you'll suddenly need to reconstruct your life goals. This can come as quite a shock. After all, it will have predominantly been just the two of you for so long, during which time you'll have had little time available to pursue or think of other goals. Don't panic. Think of the freedom available to you to create new projects or even revisit old ones. Discover your passion. You have sacrificed so much of yourself into parenting, even more so when you have been doing it solo. You deserve your reward—time to do what you desire.

We all have our unique set of talents, abilities, and strengths. You are a masterpiece; no one else remotely matches you. Your amazingness is waiting to be recognized, and the keys to your gifts are in your possession. Once you open the wrapping, you will exude abundance, attracting opportunities that will bring these gifts to life. You can then share your gifts with others. Believe in your incredibility; it will direct your purpose.

When life gets a little humdrum, you can lift out of it by creating little challenges for yourself. Set yourself some projects for the day or week that will bring you satisfaction and fulfilment. Make it so that you enhance someone else's life by giving a part of yourself. It could be that you become more intent on listening, giving someone undivided attention. You could pay someone a compliment, lend a hand, or donate some of your time. It is amazing how wonderful you feel when you brighten someone else's life. You will be rewarded in the joy you feel for having made a positive contribution to the betterment of others. The positive energy that you instigate in another human being will be transferred directly back to you. As you lift another person's mood, so too will you uplift yours. Something so simple is your act of making the world a better place.

It is so easy to cruise along inside your own little bubble, where you only have to worry about your own concerns. However, you do yourself and others an injustice by not extending yourself. Remaining in your bubble prevents you from being fully attuned to your inner calling; it silences your inner voice. Truth be known, it is your fears, anxieties, and insecurities that hold you back. Don't let procrastination determine your destiny; follow your inner voice, wisdom, and instinct—what you feel deep within the core of your being. Act upon what you believe in and trust what your heart tells you. Don't deny what feels right. Step out of your bubble and into the wider surrounds, where you can evolve.

When we pursue a purpose in life, we have something to fall back on when life slaps us around or takes a dramatic shift. It is easier to make peace with setbacks when we have personal goals to fulfil. Without a sense of purpose, we feel the full brunt of our pain during life's mishaps, big and small. With purpose, these blows are softer, and we can move forward with an excited anticipation of what lies around the corner.

Setting yourself some projects in life enhances your degree of satisfaction. You could have one or two projects on the go. Working towards your goal gives you something to look forward to in the coming weeks, months, and years. Being involved in your project divulges your talents and, in doing so, can even surprise you when hidden abilities you were unaware you possessed emerge as your project comes to fruition. You switch on an inner light that continues to burn within as you discover your authenticity. This makes you feel good—so very good.

When we think of someone achieving a major project in life, we may wonder, how he or she ever got there, secretly hoping that we too could possibly achieve something big. Know that projects begin, as well as continue through their process of completion, with bite-sized pieces, and these bite-sized pieces eventually make up the whole. Anyone can achieve anything that he or she desires; all that's required is motivation and commitment to fuel the project.

Your purpose doesn't have to be big, change the course of the world, or be earth-shattering. It just needs to be worthwhile and meaningful to you, something that allows you to exercise your talents without restrictions. It could be that you coach a basketball team, learn a new skill, or take up an art class. Your purpose may be of a personal nature—perhaps to become fitter or healthier or to devote time to your child through an important transition. Whatever it is, you will derive satisfaction knowing that you are making a positive change, and that will boost your level of happiness.

My big project has been writing this book. I was guided by my inner voice, which came through to me as a sudden revelation. Before that day, I had no intention or inclination to write. Your inner voice may present as an inkling or a strong desire; it is vital that you listen and follow the messages coming from the depths of your being—your soul. Don't ignore your ultimate wisdom, that which resides within you always. You'll better hear your inner calling when you create some space for it. Don't be afraid of fumbling in the dark; your soul will light the way. If you choose to resist the messages felt deep within your heart, your path will be concealed, and you may be left to drift aimlessly through the course of life.

When we are engaged in a project that captivates our interest, we can become in a sense of flow, oblivious to any outside disturbances, trapped in a suspended state of subconsciousness where there are no time restrictions. We are temporarily detached from our consciousness urging us to return to our mundane duties. Best of all, we are far away from all our troubles and cares. This is the epitome of living in the moment. We become so involved in the activity that the concentration involved unites us and our project as one sphere of energy; we're no longer aware of being a separate entity from the task. At this high level of interest, we become completely absorbed, involved only in the activity we are now at one with. When we are challenged and vitally involved in a project that has meaning for us, we exude a positive energy that makes us feel good, confident, and empowered, and this equates to happiness.

Sometimes we don't know what direction to take or life trips us up, and we have to make changes to our goals. Our whole reality takes a shift, and we need to let go of or modify one or more of our life goals. Don't be disheartened. You may need to put your plans on hold or redesign your goals whilst you tend to your disappointments and adapt to the disruption. Once you resurface, remain positive and keep calm. Only then will you be in touch with your intuition. And if you feel that you are about to plunge into depths unknown, trust that the universe will catch you, take you by the hand, and guide you.

We all have a story that we are living. We feature as the main character, and our identity is determined by the way we perceive ourselves and how others perceive us. Our persona is influenced by our beliefs, values, and experiences. Throughout the narrative of our life, we live segregated chapters at a time, which link together to become the whole story, at least to the point of where we are right now in our life. There are future chapters ahead, and we have a choice in how we construct them. Reflecting on previous chapters may reveal components we wish we could have shaped differently. Sometimes we just let life events happen to us without applying our values and principles. Sometimes an unexpected life event may throw us in a spin, shattering our hopes and plans. Other times, we may drift through the currents, allowing someone else to take over the oars.

You can't rewrite the chapters of your story. However, you can edit particular segments by recalling why you acted the way you did, whether you had any control over events affecting your destiny, and how decisions you made steered your goals. This allows you to highlight areas, zooming in on the choices you made and what influenced your decisions. You will then become aware of how much control you did or didn't have, how you behaved when presented with choices, and what influence others had on you. When you have this kind of perspective, you can go ahead and write your future chapters with an awareness of previous restrictions and missed opportunities. Ask yourself what goals you would like to put in place and what changes can be made to your attitude or behaviour to achieve these goals. It doesn't matter if there are things you wished you had done differently in the past. Remember that all the events in your life, even those you handled differently than you might have liked to, are instrumental in your life lessons. Plus, if you didn't have any regrets, you wouldn't have any incentive to work on transforming parts of your life now—which will give you satisfaction and meaning and a brand-new zest for living.

Some people believe they need to find their sole purpose in life. They go in search of it, thinking it will present from the outside world. They look for something that will change the course of their lives or leave an indelible imprint. These people seem to believe that we were all born with a unique purpose in life, and if we don't know what it is, we had better frantically search for it before it's too late.

I believe that our purpose comes from within, guided by our spiritual being. It involves listening in the quiet mind to what feels best and right. We don't have to prove anything to anyone else. We just need to live in truth, which will guide our actions—our sole purpose being to let our love and light shine through to the world. When we live from a place of love, we are free to spread our wings, encompassing all that life has to give us and receiving abundance in return.

Too often, we undervalue our strengths, skills, and expertise. We sit back admiring others for their achievements and cleverness, not giving ourselves deserved credit for what we too have achieved. Whatever your purpose is right at this moment, whether you are focused on one or many, it is time to applaud yourself.

Reflection

Our children will one day be grown adults, and it will be then that we will reflect on our parental role. Did we do enough? What could we have done to improve our child's upbringing? How many mistakes have we made? If we had been rated, what sort of score would we have achieved?

Parenthood is laced with moments of guilt. We all experience it. There are incidents we feel we could have prevented had we been more watchful—the baby falling off the bed or tumbling down the stairs, the toddler found playing on the road, the accidental sunburn, the child in possession of dangerous objects. The list goes on and on. There were times we didn't listen properly, times our children were sick and we ignored them because we didn't think they were feeling as badly as they make out that they were. Who hasn't accidently sent his or her child to school on one of those days? (Nurses are notorious for misdiagnosing or underestimating symptoms when it comes to their own offspring; I'm one of them). Then there were times that we yelled, were too soft or too harsh, times that we didn't spend enough time with or give enough attention to our kids, times we were too strict or not strict enough, and times when we gave too little or too much. We are human. That's the way it is. Yet that fact doesn't stop us from worrying about what effects our humanness has on our child or secretly wondering if there are more saintly parents who can hold it together better than we can.

We can't rewind time and redo our actions, so wishing that we could, won't help. What will help is the power of communication. It is paramount that we explain our behaviour and the reasons for it to our children so that they don't devise their own analogies. Really talking things through and refraining from sweeping issues under the carpet shows our respect and determination to set things straight.

We are supposedly mature adults assigned the role of parenthood, responsible for teaching, supporting, guiding, and loving our children, preparing them for independent survival and, along the way, equipping them with sufficient tools to become dependable, adaptable citizens of society.

Good parenting doesn't just happen. It takes a lot of time, energy, and self-sacrifice. We know that we can't be perfect, so we aspire to be the best parents we can be. As long as we put in our best efforts, we will have done what is required of us. How we have helped shape our children will be evident in their behaviour, their confidence, and how they fit into society.

Parenting involves on-the-job learning. We are reliant on our memories of being parented, observations of other families, and information obtained through literature and the media. We may even employ the advice of family, friends, and psychologists. Ultimately, we make the decisions and parent according to our perspective, given that our children are each unique packages, with similarities to other children but many differences as well. There is no "one for all" rule book, so we combine some of what we know and make the rest up as we believe is best suited to our situation.

Trial and error becomes the essence in which we parent. Despite practicing common sense and having a positive attitude, there are times we will make mistakes. All parents do. There's no undoing those mistakes, so there's no point in berating ourselves for having made them. When you make the wrong decision in your parenting career, acknowledge, learn, and move on. And while you're at it, take a moment to reflect on all that you have done well and praise and congratulate yourself.

Words have the power to heal, strengthen, encourage, belittle, or discriminate. Thus, we have to be careful in choosing the words we use. We must at least make the positive ones outweigh the negative. We'd be wearing halos if we didn't let any unsavoury language slip through and true saints if we never had periods of just losing it. Luckily, we know how to apologize and reaffirm that we think our children are terrific and that we love them no matter what. It is easy for a child to think otherwise if a parent is in a crappy mood, sad, or angry. How can our children feel loved if we're not displaying love? Having an underdeveloped insight, a child will be quick to assume that he or she is the cause of the parent's state of mind and so needs instant reassurance. Reinforce that your child is loved for who he or she is and that that will never change, regardless of your being temporarily angry with him or her or just in one of your moods.

Time—it's all about strengthening relationships and creating memories. Moments intertwine into periods of time continuously moving forward, eventually become past tense. It is what we do with all those interconnecting moments that later reflects how much real time we have spent with our child. So much time is consumed in taking care of a child that it's easy to forget the importance of factoring in quality presence. You could say that you are living in two different realms; a child lives completely in the moment, and an adult is preoccupied by a cascade of thoughts, intermittently regaining presence to be involved in segments of moments. Children don't have any idea that their parents aren't in the same realm and, so, often become frustrated when we have a problem finding our way out of our heads and into life as it is occurring.

Depending on how tied up we are in our thoughts, we may become annoyed at being hauled into the moment we don't have time for. We need to constantly assess our priorities to give our children significant amounts of our time where our focus is totally on them and we join together in the same realm—that of the present. The more often we do this, the less likely we are to harbour regrets when the present becomes past tense.

Although just being around your child is important, one-on-one total connectedness creates for your child a sense of feeling valued, liked, and important. This togetherness stimulates a cocktail of feel-good and love-binding hormones—oxytocin, dopamine, serotonin, and endorphins.

When these hormones flood the body, they have an uplifting effect, improving mood and feelings of well-being—a recipe for happiness.

Childhood is a short timeframe in life, and yet it's the most influential in terms of personality development. It is under our observation and guidance that our children start to lay down and establish personality traits. Temperament, although inherent, is shaped by environmental influences. It is crucial then that we as parents set the stage so as to nurture our children's budding personalities and help tailor their temperaments. This begins by forming secure attachments and by cementing these attachments with ongoing positive interactions. Our aim is to help modulate our children's behaviour to bring out the very best in them and help them reach their full potential.

How will your child evaluate his parenting when he or she is grown and reflecting back on childhood? As an adult, children will come to question the way they turned out and pinpoint significant events and influences in their lives. You will have progressed through the stages of parenthood—you'll have once sat high on the pedestal during the early childhood years, when you were adored, as you were perfect and could do no wrong, and you'll have since been kicked right off it at adolescence, when you became an obstacle to advancing independence. Finally, you will be given a complete overhaul as your adult child contemplates his or her life. Our adult children will scrutinize the good and the bad times, and our mistakes will be highlighted as they make sense out of their not-so-perfect selves. Once they have made their analyses, they will come to an understanding of your imperfections. To pass the test, your positive attributes need to override anything negative, and your grading will depend on the strength of your connection to one another, based on mutual respect, warmth, understanding, dependability, forgiveness, acceptance, and love. How you are parenting right now will eventually be assessed. You want to do well on your child's scorecard!

Conclusion

My life deviated from my original plan. To what extent can we plan life anyway? When I was young, I was intent on avoiding becoming a single parent. I thought it would be the hardest thing possible, that it would ruin my life. Well, it so happens that none of this has turned out to be true.

I will admit that, at first, single parenthood was overwhelming. I even held on to a toxic relationship for longer than I should have for the purpose of "being a family." As a single parent, I had to let go of dreams and make adjustments to my reality. This didn't come easy. I worked through a lot of issues and am pleased to say that I surprised myself in accepting my deviated path. Living as a two-member family has been better than I had imagined.

I was concerned for my child living in the smallest family unit possible. Would I be able to provide him with all that he deserved? Would he desperately miss not having a father? What about not having any siblings? These questions plagued me. I wanted to give my son everything. Yet there were some things that I couldn't, some things that I had no control over.

The feelings of inadequacy I experienced when I first became a single parent, came from a negative mindset, when in the beginning, my desired lifestyle was disrupted, and my insecurities concealed the bigger picture. I have since discovered that, when life takes a detour and you find yourself on an alternate route, new peripheral pathways appear, so long as you have an open heart and mind. All you need to do is be acceptant of what is and let go of what could have been. Have faith.

So what about my child? How does he feel about not having had his father in his life? To be honest, he does wish that he had a father and grandfather around. Yet this hasn't deterred his development on any level. I am meticulous in observing his behaviour in various social settings. I note how he interacts with his peers, how he relates to adults, and in particular his reaction to interactions between fathers and their sons. I am proud to say that he is a happy, confident child, who comfortably fits into the world, and I attribute that to the many people who have been influential in his upbringing, myself included.

We wish our children a full life no matter what. Being brought up in a single-parent family needn't preclude the possibility of this. A child is deserving of a full life in any family setting. Making that a reality simply requires the right infrastructure. Many people can provide for a child's needs, basic and psychological. These people may be parents, relatives, friends, teachers, coaches, mentors, neighbours, acquaintances, and even strangers. Each can contribute significantly to supporting a child socially and emotionally.

The connection we establish with our children begins as soon as we become parents and continues to strengthen from that moment on. Ideally, a strong, unbreakable bond will occur, particularly in the one-parent, one-child household. For this to happen, we need to be committed to our parenting role and be apt at keeping our physical, emotional, and spiritual well-being in check. This will give us the foundation required to deal with fractures when they occur. We will make mistakes. We will have regrets, and there will be times when we are in conflict with our children. This is standard in any relationship and conducive to implementing positive change.

I believe that our life experiences are so much bigger than what we perceive them to be. We are continually learning and gaining insight from these experiences, which moves us in a positive direction. Life has a set of experiences that are suited to our life purpose. We may sometimes feel left out because we don't share similar experiences with others, in particular focusing on those with a different set of circumstances—ones we may have preferred had we a choice.

Experiences don't need to be had if they are not instrumental in the life we are presently living. When you break it down, experience is a moment-by-moment encounter of events in life that are unique to each and every one of us. Even when we share an identical life experience as another person, that exact experience will have a different slant according to each individual's sensory perception of the event. Our interpretation is reliant on our senses, which in turn rely on past experiences, memories, and our present mood to determine how we view and feel about the particular experience. So even when we're sharing a walk through the park with a friend, exposed to the same sounds, scents, and sights, our individual experiences of the walk and of the park will be different. There is no point wishing we could have the same experience as another person, as that is virtually impossible. We can be in the exact same moment as someone else. However, our makeup, feelings, and conditioning will make our experience of that moment unique.

Life doesn't always go according to plan, despite our best efforts. The future is untold, so calculated events don't always eventuate. This can cause disappointment and frustration when life has been strictly scheduled. If you map your life in one direction, without accommodating for any changes, it can come as a shock when you have to take on a different course. Be positive about the situation you are in. When life takes a diversion, it's best to be excited and ready for something new. That way, you will stumble across little surprise packages, unveiling all that life has to offer.

Your experiences in life have been specifically designed for you. Accept them as challenges and see yourself blossom and flourish as your full potential is revealed. Make yourself comfortable in the life you are living, trusting in yourself and in the universe.

My wish for you is a wonderful family life and an ongoing anticipation of what's next.

Printed in the United States
By Bookmasters